My Darling
Clementine

Rutgers Films in Print
Charles Affron, Mirella Jona Affron, and Robert Lyons, editors

My Darling Clementine, John Ford, director
edited by Robert Lyons

The Last Metro, François Truffaut, director
edited by Mirella Jona Affron and E. Rubinstein

Touch of Evil, Orson Welles, director
edited by Terry Comito

The Marriage of Maria Braun, Rainer Werner Fassbinder, director
edited by Joyce Rheuban

Letter from an Unknown Woman, Max Ophuls, director
edited by Virginia Wright Wexman with Karen Hollinger

Rashomon, Akira Kurosawa, director
edited by Donald Richie

8½, Federico Fellini, director
edited by Charles Affron

La Strada, Federico Fellini, director
edited by Peter Bondanella and Manuela Gieri

Breathless, Jean-Luc Godard, director
edited by Dudley Andrew

Bringing Up Baby, Howard Hawks, director
edited by Gerald Mast

Chimes at Midnight, Orson Welles, director
edited by Bridget Gellert Lyons

L'avventura, Michelangelo Antonioni, director
edited by Seymour Chatman and Guido Fink

Meet John Doe, Frank Capra, director
edited by Charles Wolfe

Invasion of the Body Snatchers, Don Siegel, director
edited by Al LaValley

Memories of Underdevelopment, Tomás Gutiérrez Alea, director
introduction by Michael Chanan

My Darling Clementine

John Ford,
director

Robert Lyons, editor

Rutgers University Press

New Brunswick and London

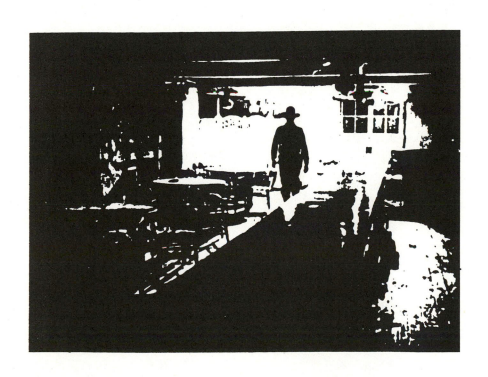

My Darling Clementine is volume 1 in the
Rutgers Films in Print Series.

Second paperback printing, 1990

Library of Congress Cataloging in
Publication Data
Main entry under title:

My darling Clementine.

   (Rutgers films in print)
   "Filmography of John Ford": p.
   Bibliography: p.
   1. Ford, John, 1894–1973.   I. Lyons,
Robert, 1935–   .   II. My darling Clementine
(Motion picture)
PN1997.M888 1984   791.43′72   83–26883
ISBN 0-8135-1050-3
ISBN 0-8135-1051-1 (pbk.)

British Cataloging-in-Publication information
available

For help in the preparation of this
volume, I wish to thank Charles
Affron, Isabelle Diaz, William Kelly,
Leslie Mitchner, Phill Niblock, the
staff of the Motion Picture Section of
the Library of Congress, and, most
especially, Bridget Gellert Lyons.

Contents

My Darling
Clementine

Introduction

Introduction

My Darling Clementine
as History and Romance

Robert Lyons

Near the beginning of John Ford's *My Darling Clementine* (1946), Wyatt Earp visits the grave of his younger brother James, shot in the back by rustlers who stole the Earps' cattle. Wyatt sits by the piled rocks that form the grave and stares at the simple marker: JAMES EARP / BORN 1864 / DIED 1882. As he looks at this inscription, he speaks to James:

> I wrote to Pa and Cory Sue [the girl James was to marry]. They're goin' to be all busted up over it. Cory Sue's young, but Pa—guess he'll never get over it. I'll be comin' out to see you regular, James. So will Morg and Virg. We're goin' to be around here for awhile. Can't tell—maybe when we leave this country, young kids like you will be able to grow up and live safe.

This moment of grief may quicken various memories in its viewers. Admirers of Ford will recall a similar scene in *Young Mr. Lincoln* (1939) in which the same actor, Henry Fonda, there as Lincoln at the grave of his dead sweetheart, also makes his desolation an occasion to commit himself to the future. They may also think more generally of Ford's reverence for the family, expressed in many of his films, and his way of making the family a source of moral strength in the face of loss or hardship. For devotees of the Western, the scene may recall other heroes called upon to avenge kinsmen killed through treachery, or still others who, through personal tragedy, become aware of a larger obligation to the rule of law.

For historians of the American West, however, the scene might provoke a very different reaction. Their recollection would be that James Earp was the eldest, not the youngest brother of Wyatt, that the youngest, Warren, was born in 1855, not 1864, that the Earps had no cattle in Tombstone, that none of them was killed in a rustling incident, and that the climactic gunfight at the O.K. Corral, linked in the film to the murder of James, occurred in 1881, not 1882. Nothing on the grave marker—despite the factuality that such objects assert—has any accuracy at all. It is understandable that Ford would recast the experience of the Earps to fit the purposes of his narrative; in order to begin a story with death, treachery, and the cutting short of a promising life, Ford introduces this particular grave in *My Darling Clementine*. But why the particular words and numbers on this gravestone? And to narrow the question further, why 1882—a date re-emphasized when Wyatt mentions it during his graveside soliloquy? To adjust the date by one year would have made no difference to the plot and would have aligned the film's dating with that of the greatest of Western shoot-outs. Instead Ford plays with facts that call for no further research than thumbing through the book on which the film is ostensibly based. His nonchalance about historical accuracy is especially striking in view of his claim, recorded in an interview with Bertrand Tavernier, that his Westerns "always" followed the historical facts, and in view of his deserved reputation as our most notable director of films about the "old West." [1]

The gravestone, then, while peripheral to the film, can be taken as evidence of Ford's ambivalent sense of the importance of history in the Western film. Ford evokes the historical actuality of precarious frontier communities, only incipiently law-abiding, that maintained tenuous connections with more cultured and established societies back East, but his ways of shaping his materials and giving them artistic coherence were those of traditional narrative romance and of earlier Western films. Actual people, places, and events are used freely to embody the themes with which romance has always been concerned: the conflict between law and lawlessness; between nature or rugged individualism on the one hand and society, culture, and art on the other; between a family's threatened extinction and its potential rejuvenation through marriage. It is Ford's sense of historical reality that makes his good, bad, or merely comic characters—identifiable partly because of their associations with the conventions of the Western—express themselves in unusually plausible language and gesture. But he also believed that people's actions could reveal qualities that were absolute: heroic, villainous, beautiful, ugly. Although he did not announce his values through such standard

1. Bertrand Tavernier, "John Ford à Paris," *Positif* 82 (March 1967):17.

iconography as a villain clothed in black (in *Clementine*, Wyatt, not Clanton, dresses in black), he did believe that Westerns "have a basically moral quality." [2] For Ford, therefore, the artist's or director's task is to shape and alter history so as to reveal its logic and meaning.

Ford's attitude to the relationship between history and the Western can be seen in his treatment of his sources. The two principal sources for the film are acknowledged in the screen credits: "Story by Sam Hellman from the book *Wyatt Earp, Frontier Marshal* by Stuart N. Lake." Lake's book, an immoderately admiring biography, whose claims were nevertheless based on historical research, had already served as the official source for two earlier films, both titled *Frontier Marshal*. Hellman's script for the second version, made in 1939, seven years before *Clementine*, is the work of a veteran Hollywood writer skillful at shaping a popular narrative.

When historical scholarship and commercial entertainment offer conflicting versions of a story, Ford almost invariably chooses the popularized version. It would be tedious and irrelevant to catalogue all the discrepancies between Lake's book and Ford's film, but a glance at Lake's account of events leading up to the gunfight at the O.K. Corral helps to clarify by contrast the structure and emphases of the film. Wyatt Earp had been in Tombstone for nearly two years before the gunfight, along with his brothers and his old friend Doc Holliday. The gunfight came as a climax to a long series of wrangles between rival business interests in Tombstone, with Earp, as part owner of a saloon and gambling hall, an involved party. Although Old Man Clanton, Earp's antagonist in the film, had been a leader of outlaws around Tombstone, he died before October 1881, the date of the battle at the corral. None of Earp's brothers had yet been killed, and the actual confrontation involved Doc Holliday with Wyatt, Morgan, and Virgil Earp on one side against two Clanton brothers, two McLowrey brothers, and Billy Claiborne. Both McLowreys and Billy Clanton were killed. Doc Holliday, unharmed in the gunfight, died of tuberculosis in a Colorado sanitarium in 1885. The Earps remained in Tombstone where, within the year, Morgan was killed and Virgil crippled in separate shootings stemming from the earlier conflict.

The second film version of *Frontier Marshal* is a far more important influence on *My Darling Clementine* in large ways and small. It provides the film with a pattern for the relationships among the four most important characters: Wyatt, Doc, the Western "bad girl" from the saloon, and the Eastern "good girl" who,

2. Bill Libby, "The Old Wrangler Rides Again," *Cosmopolitan* (March 1964):14; reprinted in this volume.

as Doc's fiancée, has followed him to Tombstone. *Frontier Marshal* contains, in slightly different versions, some of the scenes later prominent in *Clementine*: Wyatt's subduing of a drunken Indian, which leads to an offer to become the marshal of Tombstone; Doc's first appearance challenging someone in a card game at which Wyatt is a player, Doc's revival of his surgical skills in an attempt to save a life in an emergency. The earlier film also introduces comic episodes involving a traveling actor who is forced to perform for another audience than the one that expects him and who is rescued by Wyatt and Doc, scenes incorporated into *Clementine*. Ford surprisingly borrows even minor bits; one moment in *Clementine* that seems unmistakably Fordian in its comic aggression against an attractive young woman—the dunking of Chihuahua in a water trough by Wyatt—actually repeats an identical moment in *Frontier Marshal*.

Unarguably, then, *My Darling Clementine* had its genesis in the formulas and conventions of Western romance, the kind of narrative that had given Ford his start and first earned him his reputation in Hollywood. Allan Dwan, who directed the second *Frontier Marshal*, was already aware of Hollywood's tendency to romanticize Western history. He recalled with amusement the difficulties that occurred when a surviving relative of Earp's threatened to sue the producers for their misrepresentation of his life. "We never meant it to *be* Wyatt Earp. We were just making *Frontier Marshal* and that could be any frontier marshal."[3] Despite Dwan's disclaimer, his film is less effective than Ford's remake partly because of its greater fidelity to history; *Frontier Marshal* introduces too many plot complications, and some of these (most notably, the competition between two saloon owners and an elaborate scheme to hold up a stagecoach) owe their origins to Lake's biography.

Ford and his scriptwriters, Winston Miller and Samuel Engel, ignore the actual details of Earp's life whenever their inclusion would interfere with the clarity and pacing of the story. The film's coherence is enforced first of all by the confined time scheme for the action. The main events of the narrative, from Doc's arrival in the saloon to the final meeting with the Clantons, take less than three days, framed by a prologue establishing the Earps' reason for staying in Tombstone and a brief coda of Wyatt's departure. Ford's plot also establishes much tighter functional relations among characters than we find in *Frontier Marshal*. The Clantons are incriminated by Chihuahua, who thereby causes Billy Clanton to shoot her. Doc then has to operate on her, assisted by Clementine, and Chihua-

3. Peter Bogdanovich, *Alan Dwan: The Last Pioneer* (New York: Praeger, 1971):122.

hua's death leads to Doc's joining the Earps for the final gunfight. Such economical interplay of plot and character means that Ford is telling a very simple story, even by the standards of Western narrative. Yet this economy does not mean an austere narrative, one severely confined to a story of retribution. In fact, once James is dead and Wyatt has become the marshal, the film holds the Clantons in abeyance, as Winston Miller points out, while the narrative centers on Doc Holliday.[4] Only with the discovery of James's silver cross and with the death of Chihuahua do the two plots (Earp's and Holliday's—already linked by their connection to Clementine) come together in the final section of the film. The simplicity of the story line allows Ford characteristically to take his time, to include digressions such as the second barber shop scene, the scene in the Birdcage Theater, and the film's most remarkable sequence, the Sunday church meeting. These scenes, of course, are digressive only from the standpoint of plot in its most skeletal sense; they are not irrelevant to the development of the film's themes and characters, and they are crucial to its tone and atmosphere.

The other effect of the clearly defined plot is to place in sharp relief the oppositions on which the film is based. (Later, Ford perhaps recognized that such contrasts are inescapably reductive, as *The Man Who Shot Liberty Valance* [1962] demonstrates.) The conflict in Clementine is, as Wyatt says, a "family affair," with the Clantons and the Earps meeting in the first scene of the film to start the movement toward their inevitable showdown. The sense of simplicity is obtained in part through the contrasting unity of the two families; there are no disputes between brothers to complicate the plot. For the Earps, this harmony is based on familial affection, as the early scene of the four brothers around the chuck wagon makes clear. (In the shooting script, the Earps tell Old Man Clanton at their first meeting that no one is the boss in their trail gang.) The Clantons' unity, on the other hand, is imposed by the ferocity of the Old Man with his bull whip. The film's major oppositions—the Earps against the Clantons, Chihuahua against Clementine—are clearly defined and based on contrasts that the Western film had made familiar and, as was traditional, they are resolvable only by death.

Ford develops these contrasts, however, in a variety of expressive ways: in dress, in speech, in movement and gesture, and in the settings with which the characters are especially associated. The Clantons are bound to the night world where darkness conceals their treachery; they are isolated from the Tombstone community, living beyond the boundaries of the town, never participating in its

---

4. "Interview with Winston Miller," p. 141 herein.

social gatherings or daily life. They frequent the Mexican saloon, which emphasizes their separateness (and their debasement, given the racial hierarchy that the film unfortunately suggests). Chihuahua too carries the ethnic stigma of inferiority, and with it the customary traits of the Western "bad girl"—sensuality, self-indulgence, vanity, willfulness, and moodiness. Unlike Clementine, she is seen in huge, softly lit Hollywood close-ups and, although the cause of such filmic treatment may be Linda Darnell's star status, the effect is to emphasize the narcissism that is part of Chihuahua's character. In contrast, Clementine is viewed with more reserve, being seen far more frequently in medium or long shots. The film first suggests her separation from Tombstone, as she is shown waiting uncomfortably in the saloon to see Doc for the first time, or waiting alone in the Mansion House lobby for the east-bound stage the next morning. Later, she joins in the communal dance and then, in her professional role, becomes part of the effort to save Chihuahua's life.

For Ford, as for the makers of many other Westerns, these conventional contrasts served to define a kind of heroism that reflects disciplined strength and that is able, however tentatively, to associate itself with the life of the community. Wyatt's restraint and morally informed courage are obviously opposed to the unbridled violence of the Clantons. Ford himself saw Earp's significance both in his ability to accept extraordinary challenges and in his self-control and unwillingness to provoke confrontations: "They didn't have to use their guns. They overpowered the opposition with their reputations and personalities."[5] Ford's sense of the Western hero is reflected in his choice of Fonda, an actor who could evoke both idealism and intelligence, as well as an extraordinary capacity to convey his power while in repose. Wyatt rarely has to reach for his gun, even though he can do remarkable things with it when he uses it. He disposes of the drunken Indian with a rock he picks up in the street (a change from a comparable scene in *Frontier Marshal* where Wyatt wounds the Indian in a gunfight); he remains unprovoked by the weak conniving of the crooked gambler or by the arrogance of Doc Holliday's early challenges. When he does shoot, it is, classically, after the other man has drawn ("It's your play, Doc"); and then he is able to win the draw, inflicting, as he wishes, only a slight wound.

The restraint Ford admired in the behavior of his hero was also an integral part of Ford's approach to characterization in the entire film, as some of his alterations of the shooting script reveal. Ford makes Wyatt even more laconic than he

5. Libby, "Old Wrangler," p. 17.

was in the original script by cutting out the rare passages where he explains himself or offers a wisecrack. Flamboyant elements in the script are toned down in the film—Doc originally makes his first appearance in evening clothes, wearing a black cape—as is unrestrained rowdiness of the kind Ford often finds congenial—a "knock-down drag-out fight" between Clementine and Chihuahua. Similarly, Ford eliminates a good deal of the rhetorical exaggeration even of characters for whom it is appropriate: much of Doc's dialogue is sharply edited, and a long sermon by Mr. Simpson at the church service is dropped entirely. The spareness of the dialogue is a feature of Miller and Engel's original script, but the further reductions, and there are many of them, testify to Ford's conviction that speech should be secondary in film to other expressive devices.

These efforts to moderate the verbal and dramatic extravagances in the script are complemented by a similar emphasis on restraint in Ford's visual strategies in the film. Ford's reserve goes beyond his customary avoidance of dramatic camera movement, sharply accentuated close-ups, or unusual camera angles. Moments of great emotional force in the film—the deaths of James, Virgil, and Doc—are all followed by silent tableaux of the survivors, their faces in shadow, standing over the dead man. Violence in the film is presented with similar restraint: the scene in the saloon where Doc first challenges Wyatt to draw is paced quite deliberately, its drama maintained by the threat of violence that never occurs; the actual gunplay between Doc and Wyatt later in the film is rendered in a single long shot, and concluded quickly with only one shot fired. Even the climactic gun battle at O.K. Corral, where the dramatic tension is heightened by the frequent cutting, is largely concerned with the slow advance of the Earps and Holliday toward the corral and with the way in which they finally position themselves. The gunfight itself, violent though it is, takes a relatively brief time in the sequence. Furthermore, the entire scene is without music; there is only silence, interrupted by the sounds of a passing stagecoach and the horses in the corral.[6]

The most evocative images of restraint in the film are conveyed by Wyatt Earp's movements. Ford always has Fonda walk with a measured pace, and emphasizes this deliberateness by holding him in sustained long shots as he walks away from the camera. One example of this practice occurs after the meeting between the Clantons and Earp in the lobby of the Mansion House on the night of

---

6. "It's always simplicity that you should go after in any case. In the scenario, the music, the acting, the style." Ford speaks of the dangers of using too much music in this interview with Axel Madsen, "Cavalier Seul," *Cahiers du Cinéma* (October 1966):51.

James's death, a scene that concludes with Wyatt, seen from behind, walking down the long porch outside the hotel out into the darkness. A similar image occurs at the first meeting of Doc and Wyatt, when Wyatt, seen from behind, slowly walks the entire length of the Oriental Saloon to reach the end of the bar where Doc is standing. Ford contains the emotional tension of these scenes by not showing us Wyatt's face, and he emphasizes Wyatt's steadiness by the slow unbroken pace of his progress. The climactic use of the device occurs in the O.K. Corral sequence, where Wyatt, alone, walks down the main street toward the Clantons. (The film separates Wyatt from Morgan and Doc, having them slip around the back way.) Here the deliberateness of the hero's lonely walk echoes the conventions of the Western "show-down," but the ritual gesture of the challenge echoes more meaningfully because of the earlier images of walking that establish Wyatt's self-control.

Earp's characteristic movement expresses not only unhurried self-assurance; it can be extended by Ford to convey the stateliness of a formal procession. This ceremonial quality marks the walk by Wyatt and Clementine to the church service, enhanced by the hymn sung by the congregation. The sense of solemnity is established by the behavior of the central characters: Wyatt and Clementine do not converse or look to either side as they advance toward the church meeting. But what makes this moment confirm Lindsay Anderson's observation that Ford "never goes outside the immediate dramatic context to find his symbols" is the way the scene exploits Wyatt's customary movement, which here expresses the respectful admiration the hero and heroine have for each other and their willingness to be part of the town's cultural and spiritual life.[7]

Ford abandons his restraint in the chase sequence in which Wyatt pursues Doc to bring him back to Tombstone. Here Ford cuts back and forth between Doc on the stagecoach and Wyatt on horseback. The careening ride of the coach is conveyed by particularly rapid cutting, by angled shots of the coach and horses and close-ups of the coach's wheels, as well as by medium shots of Doc frantically urging the horses to go even faster. Wyatt's pursuit is shown mainly in long shots, with a corresponding decrease in intensity. Ford uses the scene to confirm an important contrast between the two men: Doc's susceptibility to impulse and emotion (the wild ride is clearly a projection of his emotional turmoil) compared with Wyatt's steadiness and control. The contrast is established early in the film, particularly in two scenes involving gamblers. The first has Doc striding through

---

7. Lindsay Anderson, "John Ford," *Cinema (Beverly Hills)* (Spring 1971): 36; reprinted herein.

the Oriental Saloon, knocking the gambler's hat off with a flourish and publicly humiliating him in front of the suddenly silent crowd. The second has Wyatt, sitting in his usual chair on the porch of the Mansion House and, without moving from his chair, looking up, or raising his voice, telling a gambler who has just stepped off the stage that the stage leaves again in thirty minutes and he should be on it. Because of his place on the porch, Wyatt is entirely in shadow and the incident is so low-key that it attracts no notice from other figures passing across the porch.

The contrast in these two scenes indicates that Ford wanted Doc's lack of control to be associated with theatricality, even though Miller's original idea of presenting him in evening clothes and cape was not used in the film. While Doc's love of Shakespeare may be part of his Eastern legacy, his love of theater is also essential to his character. He stages scenes as he stands alone at the saloon bar with the crowd as his audience, and he indulges in melodramatic gestures throughout, flinging a glass off the bar in front of the bartender, banging and kicking at Chihuahua's door, sweeping the hat off the gambler's head. Even Doc's illness has appropriate ties to the traditions of nineteenth-century melodrama, and he uses his huge white handkerchief with the skill of an actor brandishing his favorite prop, even to the moment of his death.

These traits link Doc with Chihuahua, the saloon entertainer, who also relishes playing roles in her relations with men, and whose theatricality is also connected with impulsiveness and willfulness. When she sees Doc leaving on the stagecoach, the camera follows her impetuous dash to the Mansion House along the length of Tombstone's main street, a sequence in the film's rhetoric of movement that parallels Doc's headlong ride. It reminds the audience that only Clementine is capable of matching Wyatt's measured pace in the walk to the church meeting. Their walk immediately follows the moment in the Mansion House lobby where Clementine, also faced with separation from Doc, sits quietly, wipes away a tear, and maintains her outward composure.

If self-control is an important personal value in *Clementine*, its social extension is the Western hero's commitment to law and order. Wyatt, who serves as marshal of Tombstone is, of course, the special guardian of the law. He accepts the job of marshal because of the murder of his brother, an incident that, at the beginning of many Westerns, signals a narrative of revenge and personal vindication. But Ford takes pains to shift the emphasis away from unrestrained personal vengeance and into the framework of the rule of law. In the scene at James's grave he has Wyatt vow, not to "get" the killers, but to stay with his brothers and make the territory safer and more livable. The episode at the grave is followed by a brief scene showing the three Earps in front of the town jail, their first appearance in their official role as law officers. In a change Ford has made from the shooting script, their conversation concerns their efforts to collect evidence against the Clantons. Neither script nor film ends with the Earps tracking down the Clantons, but rather with the Clantons challenging the Earps and, in so doing, invading the community of Tombstone. And in the final gunfight sequence, Ford again changes the original script so that the mayor now gives Wyatt a warrant as he leaves the jailhouse, which Wyatt then attempts to serve on Clanton before the shooting starts.

Wyatt's social involvement is not limited to his official role as marshal. At the very beginning of the film he is looking for a town so that, as he tells Old Man Clanton, he can "get a shave and a beer." At this point the alternating close-ups of Wyatt and Clanton link them as grimy, unshaven men of the open range, but while Clanton's appearance never changes, Earp's first stop in Tombstone is the barber shop. Barbering and bathing are marks of Wyatt's courtship; he welcomes Clementine to town by arranging for the hotel to heat some water for her bath, and he signals his interest in her by repairing again to the barber shop. Ford improvises some comic business around the scent which the barber sprays on Wyatt and which first his brother and then Clementine mistake for the aroma of flowers; barbering is a cultivation of nature, not a perversion of it.

The barber shop does not seem to fit entirely comfortably into the world of Tombstone, as its incongruous name "The Bon Ton Tonsorial Parlor" suggests. Tombstone is not a fully formed community as yet, only a raw town in the middle of the desert; its very rawness means that it can accommodate a hodge-podge of characters, from the sturdy and the sensible to the comic and absurd. Wyatt can appreciate this variety and participate in it: he can listen intently to Shakespeare being recited on a bar-room table, dance awkwardly but enthusiastically at a church social, and play his cards at poker better than a professional gambler. As a result, he also sees the function of the law as protecting the diverse aspects of life in Tombstone; he is mainly concerned with keeping people from being bullied or "run out of town." (Wyatt's sense of diversity, it must be noted, has significant racial limitations; he handles the drunkenness of Indian Charlie or the cheating of Chihuahua differently from similar offenses by other characters.)

Running people out of town is something Doc Holliday likes to do, and both Doc's challenges to Wyatt in Tombstone arise from that habit. Doc has no real ties to Tombstone; he comes and goes and, wherever he goes, he brings his own sense of the rules with him. While Wyatt admires Doc's courage and commitment to personal honor, he refuses to allow Doc to ignore legal authority. The conflict between them is clearest when Doc confronts Clementine in the hotel dining room to demand why she has not already left town, since he has told her to do so. The scene, both visually and thematically, echoes Doc's earlier expulsion of the gambler, but here it is much clearer that Doc's rules are really pure egotism, and Wyatt rightfully intervenes. Even at the end of the film, when he seems to have allied himself with legal action, Doc's role in the gunfight is blurred; his unstated motives for joining in seem to combine a desire to avenge the killing of Chihuahua and a suicidal urge—emblematized in his fatal illness—to escape the divisions within his own nature. While, unlike Wyatt, Doc can never be imagined acting as a representative of the citizens of Tombstone, he is, however, sharply differentiated from such outlaw figures as Old Man Clanton. Doc does have social ties, but they are with Boston, a society from which he is in flight. His most attractive qualities—his cultivation, his gentlemanliness, and what remains of his professional skill as a doctor—are all legacies of the East; his relationship to the West—where he wants to be without ties or permanent social commitments—is entirely self-destructive.

The conflict Doc Holliday embodies between East and West sets him at the center of a spectrum of characters in the film who represent, in different ways, the social values of Eastern and Western America and the possibilities of community between these two very different cultures. The differences are signaled verbally, and the spectrum ranges from the barbaric monosyllables of the Clantons to the fulsome rhetoric of the actor Thorndyke, whose speech is a collection of ill-assorted literary snippets. The scene in the Mexican saloon where Thorndyke and the Clantons come together dramatizes their mutual loathing as well as their separate inadequacies. Against these extremes, Wyatt and Clementine bring East and West into shared communication and shared admiration. She speaks with articulateness and formality, he with laconic casualness. Ford has always been uncomfortable with the formalities of educated speech, and Miller's "Eastern" conversations between Doctor John Holliday and Clementine have a deliberately stilted and archaic air: "The man you once knew is no more. There is not a vestige of him left." While the film is not interested in denigrating the Easterner—after all, Wyatt is attracted to both of these characters—Ford does make clear through the silences that dominate all his major scenes that Eastern fluency can never encompass the significant moments in experience. "There are so many things I wanted to say, and . . . now nothing seems appropriate" is Clementine's final and graceful submission to the Fordian world.

Clementine and Wyatt also share a sense of the importance of communal life;

both bring the professional skills they have learned in their own cultures to the service of Tombstone. They do not speak to each other of their common beliefs and personal feelings, except very briefly and elliptically in the final scene, but their attitudes are expressed by their participation in the social rituals of the new community. Ford eliminates a scene in the shooting script in which Doc escorts Clementine back to the hotel after their first meeting; instead, after Doc tells Clementine to take the next stage back East, the scene dissolves to Doc entering the hotel room alone. The Sunday church scene thus becomes the only one in which Clementine moves escorted by a man, and that formal walk comes directly after a scene in Doc's bedroom in which Doc agrees to stage a wedding breakfast for Chihuahua. The scenes present the formation of two different kinds of bonds. The point is not that Wyatt and Clementine lack strong feeling, but that they express it through the forms of social ritual that are meaningful to the community as well as to themselves. Doc, on the other hand, makes no mention of calling the minister or mayor; his wedding plans concentrate on dress and decor for a wedding breakfast.

The values of community are closely related to the sense of social harmony that the film evokes. At no point do we feel that darker forces are endemic to the community: the Clantons are clearly outsiders, and the other prominent figures associated with disruption, Doc and Chihuahua, are simultaneously ennobled and eradicated through death. When the Earps first ride into Tombstone, the town's social energies are located in the raucous life of its saloons, but in the latter part of the film social pleasures occur in less raffish contexts—the church site, the hotel dining room, and even the saloon itself, which undergoes a sobering transformation when Wyatt converts it into an operating room. The town is represented by decent and honest men (the mayor and the deacon) whose authority is civil and religious, not the law of the gun. At the same time, the great American gulf, as Ford sees it, between East and West is virtually overcome; if the two worlds are not joined in marriage, they certainly arrive at mutual respect and admiration.

Other gulfs, however, are resolved by exclusion, not integration. Earp sends Indian Charlie out of Tombstone with a kick in the pants and threatens the same quick exit to Chihuahua ("back to the reservation," he says, as if Indians and Mexicans were interchangeable) when he dunks her in the horse trough. Both these scenes of comic humiliation deny their victims even the dignity of adversaries; Indians and Mexicans are simply subordinates, not part of the company of "decent citizens" who Wyatt says are always free to stay in Tombstone as long as they wish. Such racial complacency is the underside of Ford's strong sense of community.

However narrow the social canvas, the conception of community manifests itself in the film in many ways besides Ford's treatment of narrative and character. The remarkably realistic Tombstone set, whose construction in Monument Valley was supervised by Ford, itself testifies to the director's concern for the significance of such Western settlements. His characteristic preference for shots other than individual close-ups—his way of having figures cluster together in moments of rejoicing, suffering, or death—reinforces a sense of human interdependence. Ford's comment that he wanted to end *My Darling Clementine* differently, with Wyatt settling down in Tombstone and marrying his girl, expresses not merely a desire to fit the prescription for a Hollywood ending, but a recognition of how powerfully this film asserts Ford's belief in community.[8]

Nevertheless, the film's actual ending, which seems right to most viewers, shows that its commitment to community (let alone domesticity), while powerful, is not unqualified. Wyatt takes leave of Clementine with a kiss on the cheek and a handshake, not the full embrace of a committed suitor, and his promise to return is couched in language that expresses more caution than determination. The ending confirms a doubleness that is part of the tradition of Western narrative. As a hero of Western romance, Wyatt stands apart; his judgment is as unerring as his shooting eye, and except for his charming awkwardness as an admirer of Clementine, he is always in command of himself and of the situation he faces. Ford admires such a man but associates his special qualities with isolation, with an inwardness and separateness that are inescapable aspects of his strength and moral assurance. As Wyatt Earp, Henry Fonda recalls earlier Ford heroes he played, most particularly Ford's greatest American hero, Abraham Lincoln. The links between the two characters are evident not only in the two grave scenes, mentioned earlier, but in comparable sequences in which Fonda's self-conscious dancing suggests the tentative relation that each character has with his community. Lincoln will save his society, but, as his self-imposed isolation in the final frames of the film suggests, he can never be fully part of it, since the hero can never comfortably disappear within the community as just another one of its members.

In *My Darling Clementine*, Ford's awareness of Earp's special role emerges in the expressive power of many shots of Wyatt alone: sitting in his chair on the

8. Quoted in Andrew Sinclair, *John Ford* (New York: Dial Press, 1979):130.

porch of the Mansion House, visiting the grave of his brother, walking away from the camera at the end of several scenes, and walking in isolation toward the Clantons as the confrontation at the corral approaches. It emerges also in Wyatt's ways of modifying the social functions of speech—first by his silences, then by his laconic remarks, and finally by the mixture of private rumination and public utterance when he speaks at length. Whether he is talking to the Clantons or to Clementine, Wyatt most often leaves us with the sense of things still unspoken or only obliquely referred to.

What Ford's film finally does, then, is blur the distinction between the hero as the possessor of an individual moral code and the hero as the embodiment of acceptable social values. Wyatt is, on the one hand, the ex-marshal who has no intention of stopping in Tombstone, the older brother intent on finding the murderer in what is a "family affair," the man who walks alone down the porches and streets of Tombstone, and the moralist who, after righting the wrongs in the town, rides away without his girl. But he is also the new marshal who makes sure that decent citizens are not bullied or driven away, the shy lover who joins the dancing and carves the roast at a Sunday dinner, the frequenter of barber shops who worries about how his hat sits on his head. At the end of the film, Morgan has already left, so when Wyatt rides away, we see the last of him somewhere between Clementine and his brother. But here Ford's camera does not follow Wyatt from behind, as it has in so many earlier moments; instead it remains with Clementine, who has already declared her allegiance to the town of Tombstone.

When Ford voiced his displeasure many years later with the ending of *My Darling Clementine* (changed against his wishes, he claimed, by his studio), it was because the ending violated history; the historical Wyatt, he said, stayed in Tombstone. But the original shooting script contains the ending we now have, and Winston Miller does not remember Ford objecting to it. It is more likely that an older and more pessimistic Ford saw *Clementine* as too committed to the idea of new communities and the evolution of the West and that, as was his habit, he supported his aesthetic and moral perceptions by invoking history.[9] Just as with

9. In his last Western, *Cheyenne Autumn* (1964), Ford returned to the characters of Earp and Holliday, now transformed into middle-aged card players who see life with cynical detachment. They appear in a broadly comic vignette, set in a saloon, and their world is peopled by madams, card sharks, and bar-room buffoons. Their casual hedonism is unrelated to the main narrative of the film, the tragic story of the heroic sufferings of displaced Cheyenne Indians. The inclusion of the Earp–Holliday sequence (it is not in Ford's source material and it has no historical validity) suggests that Ford intends the scene as an ironic commentary and coda to the vision he embodied in *My Darling Clementine*.

the gravestone of James Earp, Ford asserts the importance of history—his own, in this case, as well as that of the West—at the same time that he reinvents it. For Ford, the past never determined the present, and therefore the specific details of the past never needed to be verified or reproduced exactly. But he turned to history repeatedly for patterns of heroism, cowardice, wisdom, or irrationality because historical subjects could be rendered authoritatively but freely, without the multiple associations and equivocal interpretations that surround events in contemporary life. As Winston Miller says, "Everyone knows about O.K. Corral, but nobody knows what actually went on there."

In *My Darling Clementine*, Ford reveals his confidence about America by emphasizing Earp's Western values tempered by respect for those of the East and by showing the future of Tombstone full of the promise evoked in the Sunday morning scene, where flag, church steeple, natural landscape, and dancing townspeople all fit compatibly within the images he creates. The pictorial beauty that marks the film, a quality that led the critic Robert Warshow to dismiss it as too "soft," is the most compelling evidence of the sense of a harmonious world that shapes Ford's vision here. Admittedly, Ford's optimism is tinged with melancholy; the old dichotomies of the Western romance are never entirely put aside, and audiences cannot dispel the after-image of Wyatt Earp moving slowly away from them, elusive and enigmatic. Nevertheless, *My Darling Clementine* is ultimately a film of reconciliation in which Ford uses the historical legend of Wyatt Earp to create an affirmation, perhaps his most confident affirmation, of American moral values and social purpose.

John Ford: A Biographical Sketch

John Ford was born Sean O'Feeney in Cape Elizabeth, Maine, in 1895, the thirteenth child of an Irish immigrant family. After graduating from high school, he went to Hollywood in 1913 and began working for his brother, an actor-writer-director who had taken the name Francis Ford. Sean O'Feeney became Jack (later John) Ford, serving his apprenticeship under his brother as a stunt man and bit player, and eventually as an assistant director.

Ford's early career in Hollywood is difficult to document precisely, since most of the films he was involved with at that time have not survived, but the first film he directed was probably *The Tornado* (1917). He specialized in Westerns and made them skillfully, quickly, and efficiently; in 1919, for example, Ford directed fifteen films. His greatest success during the silent period, *The Iron Horse* (1924), chronicled the race between the Union Pacific and Central Pacific to build the first transcontinental railroad line. The film, far more elaborate and expensive than Ford's usual assignments, established him as an important Hollywood director.

During the 1930s, Ford had a number of successes, working mainly for Twentieth Century-Fox. His most celebrated achievement, a highly unconventional project by Hollywood standards, was an adaptation of Liam O'Flaherty's *The Informer* (1935). He coaxed and bullied the studio into allowing him to make the film, and it won him his first Academy Award. *The Informer* was written by Dudley Nichols, who collaborated with Ford on many of his most important works during the next decade. Ford finished the 1930s with an extraordinary burst of creative energy. Between 1939 and 1941 he made seven films and among them were five that are usually ranked among his best work: *Stagecoach* (1939), *Young Mr. Lincoln* (1939), *Drums Along the Mohawk* (1939), *The Grapes of Wrath* (1940), and *How Green Was My Valley* (1941). The last two again won Ford Academy Awards; more significantly, the first four of these films testify to his deep involvement with American themes and with the significance of the American past. Ranging in time from the Revolution to the Depression, these titles demonstrate that Ford's interest in Westerns was part of his broader interest in American character as revealed through American history.

Ford's Hollywood career was interrupted when he served as Chief of the U.S. Navy's Field Photographic Branch during World War II. While on military service he made a documentary about the battle of Midway and a feature film, *They Were Expendable* (1945), dealing with the navy's PT boat and the man who introduced it into combat. Ford returned to civilian life in 1945, and his first film of the postwar period was *My Darling Clementine* (1946).

Shortly after the war, Ford formed his own production company with Merion C. Cooper, a move that made him relatively free to work on projects of his own choice. Nevertheless, his films of the 1950s and 1960s tended to concentrate on familiar subjects—the Western and films with Irish or Irish-American settings. One of the latter group, *The Quiet Man* (1952), won Ford his fourth and last Academy Award.

Ford's later films reemphasized his delight in sentiment and in masculine horseplay and knockabout humor, while resolutely ignoring the social realism and the attention to contemporary life that marked the work of many postwar American directors. He did not, however, simply drift into escapist entertainments. His great Westerns of the period, most notably *The Searchers* (1956), *The Man Who Shot Liberty Valance* (1962), and *Cheyenne Autumn* (1964), document the gradual diminution of Ford's faith in American standards and values.

The final years of Ford's life were a struggle against a series of illnesses. He was forced to turn over one of his cherished projects, a film about the early life of the Irish playwright Sean O'Casey, to another director after a few days' shooting. The film that proved to be his last, *Seven Women* (1966), served as an ironic conclusion for a director whose work had portrayed a largely masculine world. Ford died of cancer in Palm Springs, California, in 1973.

My Darling
Clementine

My Darling Clementine

The shooting script of *My Darling Clementine* was written by Samuel G. Engel and Winston Miller and was completed in March, 1946. This script was John Ford's text when he began to film the story in the late spring of 1946. As Winston Miller explains in the interview appearing in this volume, Ford had already taken a very active role in the development of this script; nevertheless, he made many changes while filming. The film as audiences now know it, reflected by the continuity script, differs from the shooting script in many ways, most of them very minor, some of them quite significant. Notes on the Shooting Script (printed at the end of the continuity script and keyed to the superscript numbers therein) discuss these differences. Limitations of space (and some regard for the reader's patience) prevent publishing all the variant passages in the shooting script, but the notes describe those variations that shed some light on Ford's purposes and methods. Furthermore, any scene in the shooting script but not in the film is described; any scene in the film but not in the shooting script is noted. In addition, since the Sunday morning sequence is probably the most celebrated section of the film and since it diverges considerably from the version in the shooting script, that part of the shooting script is reprinted in its entirety.

The continuity script that follows represents the version of *My Darling Clementine* that was given theatrical release in November 1946. The editor has transcribed the dialogue and attempted to recreate the visual experience of the film. The print used as the

source for this text is one owned by
the Library of Congress.

The abbreviations used to describe
camera distance follow the usual
conventions:

CU   close-up
MS   medium shot
LS   long shot
MTS medium two shot

Credits and Cast

Director
John Ford

Producer
Samuel G. Engel

Screenplay
Samuel G. Engel and Winston Miller,
from a story by Sam Hellman, based
on the book *Wyatt Earp, Frontier
Marshal* by Stuart N. Lake

Production Company
Twentieth Century-Fox

Director of Photography
Joseph P. McDonald

Art Directors
James Basevi, Lyle R. Wheeler

Set Decorators
Thomas Little, Fred J. Rode

Costumes
Rene Hubert

Music
Cyril Mockridge

Musical Direction
Alfred Newman

Orchestral Arrangements
Edward Powell

Special Photographic Effects
Fred Sersen

Sound
Eugene Grossman, Roger Heman

Editor
Dorothy Spencer

Assistant Director
William Eckhardt

Technical Advisor
Wyatt Earp

Location
Monument Valley, Arizona/Utah

Process
Black and white

Length
Ninety-seven minutes

Release Date
November 1946

Wyatt Earp
Henry Fonda

Chihuahua
Linda Darnell

Doc Holliday
Victor Mature

Old Man Clanton
Walter Brennan

Virgil Earp
Tim Holt

Morgan Earp
Ward Bond

Clementine Carter
Cathy Downs

Granville Thorndyke
Alan Mowbray

Billy Clanton
John Ireland

Ike Clanton
Grant Withers

Mayor
Roy Roberts

Kate Nelson
Jane Darwell

John Simpson
Russell Simpson

Old Dad
Francis Ford

Mac, the Bartender
J. Farrell MacDonald

James Earp
Don Garner

Barber
Ben Hall

Hotel Clerk
Arthur Walsh

Theater Owner
Don Barclay

François
Louis Mercier

Sam Clanton
Micky Simpson

Phin Clanton
Fred Libby

Gambler
Earl Foxe

Luke, the Marshal
Harry Woods

Indian Charlie
Charles Stevens

Stagecoach Drivers
Jack Pennick, Robert Adler

Simpson's Sister
Mae Marsh

Guitar Player
Aleth 'Speed' Hansen

Accordion Player
Danny Borzage

Piano Player
Frank Conlan

The Continuity Script

*Fade in to extreme long shot of parched Arizona landscape, with mesas tower-
ing in the distance and flat, scrubby land in the foreground. Music accompanies the scene on the soundtrack.* A herd of cattle emerges from lower
ground onto the flatlands and slowly crosses the frame from right to left. Three
long shots of the herd and the mounted cowboys working it, with each shot
progressively closer, alternate with three medium shots of individual cowboys
on horseback, each occupied with keeping the herd under control. The cowboys are three of the Earp brothers; successively we see James, Morgan, and
Virgil. This last shot of Virgil is followed by a similar shot of Wyatt Earp, held
somewhat longer as Wyatt steadies his horse and turns in the saddle, watching
the cattle.[1]*

*An extreme long shot of the herd seen from a distance and at a somewhat
higher elevation. A buckboard pulled by two horses moves into the foreground
and stops. The two men in the buckboard, backs to the camera, look out at
the herd.*

*Medium shot of Old Man Clanton, the driver, a wizened, hard-bitten old-
timer with a whip in his hand. Seated next to him is his eldest son, Ike, a big,
bullish man. Both study the herd speculatively.*

IKE: Texas?
CLANTON *(shaking his head)*: Chihuahua steers.

*Return to previous long shot, as Wyatt rides up from the herd toward the
buckboard.[2]*

CLANTON: Howdy.
WYATT: Howdy.

Medium shot of Clanton and Ike.

---

*Only on rare and brief occasions does Ford use music that is not produced by characters within
the story. Such background music will be noted only when it is prominent.

CLANTON: My name's Clanton. This is my boy, Ike. My oldest boy.

Medium shot of Wyatt on his horse.

WYATT: Any sweetwater up beyond?

CLANTON (MTS): Yeah. Two or three miles straight up the trail. *(He again looks over the herd.)* Cattle look pretty scrawny.

WYATT (MS): Yeah. Me 'n' my brothers we're trailin' 'em on to California.

CLANTON (MTS): If ya ain't got 'em committed to no shipper, I'll take 'em offten your hands.

WYATT (MS): Not interested.

CLANTON (MTS): Make you a good offer. Pay you in silver three dollars a head.

WYATT (MS): Nope.

CLANTON (MS): Might raise it to five dollars silver.

WYATT (MS): Paid more than that in Mexico.

CLANTON (MS): They'll be a sorry lookin' lot by the time they get to California, son.

WYATT (CU): They'll feed out when we get to grass country. *(Cut to MS of Clanton.)* Sure is rough lookin' country. *(Back to CU of Wyatt.)* Ain't no cow country. Mighty different where I come from. What do they call this place?

CLANTON (CU): Just over the rise there's a big town. Called Tombstone. Fine town.

WYATT (CU): Tombstone! Yeah, I heard of it. Well, me and my brothers might ride in there tonight. Get ourselves a shave, maybe . . . glass o' beer.

CLANTON (MTS): Yeah, you'd enjoy yourselves. Wide-awake, wide-open town, Tombstone. Get anything you want there.

WYATT (MS): Thank you.

Long shot from behind the wagon, as Wyatt starts to ride back to the herd.
Medium shot of Ike, who turns to look at his father.
Medium shot of Clanton, whose mouth tightens and eyes narrow as he stares after Wyatt.
Medium two shot of the Clantons as the old man lifts his whip and snaps it forward.
Long shot from behind Wyatt as he rides down toward the herd. The camera holds as Wyatt approaches the herd and one of his brothers riding at its edge.

Dissolve into night scene with long shot of three Earp brothers eating supper, sitting around a campfire, while James stands by the chuck wagon to the right. They are in the midst of the open space of the flatlands, with their cattle grazing behind them.
    Medium shot of Morgan and Wyatt seated behind the campfire, holding plates and eating.

MORGAN: James, this is mighty fine chow. One of these days you're gonna be as good a cook as Maw.

Medium shot of James and Virgil standing at the back of the chuck wagon.

JAMES *(embarrassed)*: Well, I'm learnin', tryin'.
VIRGIL: That's what I keep tellin' him. Cory Sue ain't marryin' him 'cause he's so pretty, but 'cause he's such an awful good cook.

James has a small cloth bag in his hand. From it he takes an object hanging on a chain.
    Extreme close-up of a distinctive looking Mexican cross in James's palm.

MORGAN (MTS *with Wyatt*): There goes that Chingadera again.

Medium shot of Virgil and James at the chuck wagon.

VIRGIL: That sure is a mighty pretty piece of brass.
JAMES *(incredulous)*: Brass? That's solid silver. Twenty-five American dollars' worth of solid silver. Ain't it, brother Wyatt?

Medium shot of Wyatt and Morgan, sanding their plates to clean them off.

WYATT: It sure is, James, don't let him fool ya. It'll look mighty pretty in them yaller curls of Cory Sue.
JAMES (MTS *with Virgil*): Ain't that the truth, now. *(He breathes on the cross, in order to keep polishing it.)*

Medium two shot of Morgan and Wyatt. Morgan gets up, moves out of frame right, leaving Wyatt drinking coffee. Wyatt rises.

WYATT: Let's mount up. If we're goin' to town, let's get goin'.[3]

Medium shot of the back of the chuck wagon, now with Morgan having joined James and Virgil. Morgan takes the cross and chain from James and holds it out in front of him.
    Medium shot of the cross dangling in the light.

MORGAN *(off-screen)*: Twenty-five dollars gold. By golly *(cut to MTS of Morgan and James)* you sure got a bargain.

Morgan gives the cross back to James and leaves left, as James smiles appreciatively.
    Medium shot of Wyatt finishing his coffee. Virgil and Morgan cross in front of him, passing in and out of frame from right to left.

MORGAN *(to horses, off-screen)*: Whoa, there, whoa!

Medium shot of James, still standing by the chuck wagon.

VIRGIL *(off-screen)*: So long, James.
WYATT *(off-screen)*: So long, James.
JAMES: So long, Wyatt, Morgan. So long, Virgil.

Camera remains on James, smiling and looking off-screen after his departing brothers.

Dissolve to the three Earps riding toward camera in long shot across the Arizona flatlands. The sky is heavily clouded and threatening; moonlight cuts through the clouds in dramatic patterns. The camera pans with them as they pass an unhitched covered wagon, a marker of the outskirts of Tombstone. The Earps rein in their horses to survey what lies ahead. We see in the middle distance the outlines of more covered wagons, then the buildings and scattered lights of Tombstone beyond. Sounds of laughter and music can be heard faintly from the town.

VIRGIL: There it is. Tombstone.
WYATT: Let's go.

The Earps spur their horses and ride rapidly away from the camera and toward the town.

Dissolve to a long shot looking across the main street of Tombstone.[4] *The street has buildings only on one side, facing out across the street toward the open country. The camera looks at the buildings and follows the Earps as they ride slowly along the street. Behind them, most of the buildings are lighted; doors are wide open, and the light streams out onto the long porches with their overhangs that run the length of the block. Sounds of loud music, laughter, and raucous conversation seem to come from everywhere. The porches and even the street seem crowded; horses and pack mules move along the street or are tied to hitching posts at the side. The camera pans with the Earps as they pass the one cross street in Tombstone and continue just beyond it.*

Long shot from the porch as the Earps pull in their horses and dismount. They step up on the sidewalk just beyond the corner of the cross street, while the noise continues. Most of the porch area is in half-light, except for a wooden barber's pole with a sign "Baths" below it, all highlighted by a bright panel of light from a shop window. The camera follows the Earps as Virgil crosses the porch to look in the window.

Long shot of Wyatt as he stands in front of the barber's pole; he is joined by Morgan.

Long shot of the crowded saloon, seen from just outside and above the swinging doors at the entrance. The saloon is now identified as the principal source of the noise and laughter.

Medium shot of Wyatt and Morgan on the sidewalk, now joined by Virgil. All three look slightly dazed, unaccustomed to the turbulence of the town. They take one or two steps toward the camera and the source of the light. Wyatt, in the center, is stroking his beard.

BARBER *(off-screen)*: Good evening, gentlemen.

Medium shot of the barber, a small, rather innocuous man, leaning with one arm against the barber's chair in his shop, wearing a white jacket, carrying a towel on his arm.

BARBER: Welcome to the Bon Ton Tonsorial Parlor.

Return to medium shot of the Earps.

WYATT: Barber shop?

Long shot from inside the shop. The barber now stands beside his chair, the Earps in the doorway.

BARBER: Well, if you want to call it that.

The Earps walk in, while the barber prepares his covering cloth.

BARBER: What can I do for ya?

The Earps, grubby and unshaven, all stop and stare at him in disbelief.

WYATT *(after a pause, deliberately)*: Shave.
BARBER: Haircut?
WYATT *(settling himself in the barber's chair)*: Shave.
BARBER *(putting the cover over Wyatt)*: We give baths, too.
WYATT *(doggedly)*: Shave.

The barber moves the lever to tilt the chair back. Instead the chair moves with a sudden lurch, almost throwing Wyatt to the floor.

BARBER *(apologetically)*: I don't know how to work it so good. Only had it a week. Come all the way from Chicago.

Long shot from behind the barber's chair. In the foreground, Wyatt peers over the side of the chair, to see if it will stay upright. In the background, the barber pours hot water into his bowl and begins to stir up a lather.

BARBER: Say, you fellas miners?
WYATT: Nope.
BARBER: Prospectors? Huh?

Brief medium shot of Virgil sitting and reading a newspaper.[5]

WYATT *(with slight exasperation)*: Cattlemen!

Return to previous shot. Wyatt is now leaning back in the chair so that he is almost horizontal and the barber approaches him with the lathering bowl.

WYATT: Just passing through here. *(more emphatically)* Shave, please.

Long shot from directly behind the barber's chair. Gunfire is heard and two bullet holes appear in the barber's wall mirror, directly in front of the chair. Morgan is standing there with his face close to the mirror, trimming his beard. The barber, Morgan, and Wyatt whirl around to face the camera. The barber quickly turns and leaves the frame to the left.
    Long shot from behind and to the right of the barber's chair. The barber leaves through some swinging doors in the background. Wyatt raises himself up in the chair.

WYATT: Hey, barber!

Wyatt gets up and goes after the barber, still wearing his barber's cloth. As he reaches the swinging doors, another shot hits a pot of water on the stove, sending up a geyser of steam. Wyatt turns back into the room and the three Earps stand looking at the stove for a moment.

WYATT: What kind of a town is this? *(turning and heading toward the doors)* Barber!!

Medium shot looking across the shop in front of the barber's chair. Virgil and Morgan duck as more shots are heard and objects behind them on shelves near the mirror begin to shatter.
    Long shot of the porch outside the shop. People are running past as Wyatt first crouches down on the porch as more shots are heard; when he straightens up and looks around, the porch is empty. He walks determinedly out into the street and out of the frame to the right, still with lather on his face and carrying the barber's cloth.
    Long shot of the front door of Kate Nelson's "Ladies' Boarding House," Tombstone's brothel. More shots ring out and several women in dance-hall costumes, silhouetted in the bar of light from the doorway, come bursting out into the street, shrieking with fright. As they disappear out of the frame, a

single figure can be seen indistinctly inside the building, staggering and shoot-
ing a gun in the air.
    Medium shot of a group of townspeople in the street. The Mayor is facing
the Marshal, with other men and Kate Nelson crowded around behind them.[6]

MAYOR: Luke, you know your duty. You and your marshals go on in there and
    get him out.
MARSHAL: That's Indian Charlie in there drunk, and I ain't committin' suicide
    on myself. *(He takes off his badge and hands it to the Mayor.)*
FIRST DEPUTY: Me neither. *(He does the same.)*
SECOND DEPUTY: No, sir. I ain't a-goin' in there. *(He too turns in his
    badge.)*

Wyatt appears from the left, pushing into the circle.

WYATT: What kind of a town is this, anyway? *(to Kate Nelson)* 'Scuse me,
    ma'am. *(to Mayor)* A man can't get a shave without gettin' his head blowed
    off. *(to Marshal)* You're the Marshal, ain't you? Why don't you go in and
    get that drunk Indian out of there?
MARSHAL: Why don't you go and get him out yourself?
WYATT: They ain't payin' me for it.
MARSHAL: And they ain't payin' me enough either. *(He turns and leaves.)*

More shots are heard and everyone in the group flinches and ducks down.
    Long shot of the boarding house entrance; the Indian is framed in the lighted
doorway, a gun in each hand, firing and letting our war whoops.
    Return to previous shot as Wyatt and the others slowly straighten up. Wyatt
looks impatient and irritated; he hands the barber's cloth to the Mayor and
heads toward the camera and out of the frame.

KATE NELSON *(calling after him)*: Young man, you be careful!

Long shot of the boarding house doorway. Wyatt, seen from behind, stops to
pick up a stone, crosses quickly in front of the doors, kicks one door shut, and
then runs up a set of outside stairs that lead to a second-floor window.
    Medium long shot of the staircase; as Wyatt disappears up the stairs, he is

*followed by another burst of gunfire from the Indian. A window at the foot of
the stairs is blown out and a fire starts inside.*

   *Long shot looking up the staircase. Wyatt is at the top, opening the second-
floor window. As he swings one leg over the sill, screams are heard from inside.*

WYATT *(as he climbs in, still holding the stone in one hand)*: It's all right,
   ladies.

*Long shot from outside the saloon doors. The doors slowly swing open as
people inside, silent now, peer out into the street.*

   *Medium shot of three old codgers in the street, leaning forward expectantly,
waiting for the excitement. One, Old Dad, has his fingers in his ears, to shut
out the gunfire.*

OLD MAN: I don't blame old Luke. I wouldn't go in there, either.

Medium shot of the Mayor, Kate Nelson, and one of the deputies waiting tensely. A loud thud is heard off-screen.

Long shot of the boarding house entrance, with the camera tilted down toward floor level. The lower half of a man comes into the frame walking through the doorway. He is leaning forward, dragging an unconscious man along the floor by his heels.

Long shot from the boarding house entrance out into the street. Wyatt is dragging the Indian toward the townspeople. He comes up to the Mayor and drops the Indian's feet in front of him.

Medium long shot of Wyatt and the Mayor surrounded by townspeople.

WYATT: What kind of a town is this, anyway! Selling liquor to Indians! *(He pulls the Indian to his feet; the Indian holds his head and groans; Wyatt examines the top of his head.)* I put a knot on his head bigger than a turkey's egg. Indian, get out of town and stay out! *(Wyatt swings the Indian around, pushes him away, and kicks him in the pants. The Indian staggers out of the frame on the left.)*
MAYOR: How'd you like to stay on here. As Marshal, I mean.
WYATT: Nope. *(begins to look around, over the crowd)* Barber!!
MAYOR: Two hundred a month goes with this badge.
WYATT: Not interested. I'm just passin' through tryin' to get me a relaxin' little shave. *(takes the barber's cloth back from the Mayor)*
MAYOR: We'll make it two fifty.
WYATT: Not interested. Hey, Mr. Bon Ton! *(He spots the barber and breaks through the crowd, followed by the Mayor.)*

Medium shot follows Wyatt as he strides up to the sidewalk and grabs the barber by the arm. The barber still has the lather bowl and brush in his hand. Wyatt's face is still covered with lather.

WYATT *(with great emphasis)*: Shave, please! *(He starts to push the barber toward the shop.)*
MAYOR: Well, we sure want to thank you, Mr. er . . .
WYATT: Earp. Wyatt Earp.
MAYOR *(reacting to the name)*: You're not by any chance the Marshal from Dodge City?
WYATT *(turning and propelling the barber before him down the sidewalk)*: Ex-Marshal.

Wyatt and the barber turn into the lighted doorway of the barbershop as the Mayor stands in the foreground and watches them disappear.

Fade in to a long shot of the three Earps riding together over open land late at night. It is now pouring rain. They ride toward the camera, then pull up their horses directly before the camera.

WYATT: The cattle's gone!

Long shot of the chuck wagon standing deserted, part of its canopy left open to the downpour.
    Medium shot of a kettle on a tripod over the extinguished camp fire.
    Close-up of cooking pots and plates from supper left on the lowered tailgate of the wagon.
    Long shot of a horse left unattended, its reins hanging slack to the ground. In the foreground, just by the side of the horse and parallel to it, is a man's body.
    Close-up of the head and one hand of the man on the ground—it is James Earp. Rain splashes in the puddles around his head.
    Long shot of the three brothers on their horses.

WYATT: James!

They spur their horses toward the camera and out of the frame on the left.
    Another close-up of James's head and hand.

WYATT *(off-screen)*: James!

Long shot as the brothers ride into the frame from the right; they pull up and Virgil quickly dismounts.
    Long shot of the horse and James's body. Virgil enters the frame and crosses to stand at the foot of the body. Wyatt follows him and kneels by James's side.
    Medium shot of Wyatt kneeling by his brother. He lays his hands on James's back and his uncovered head.
    Long shot of all three brothers, for Morgan has now joined them and is standing at the head of the body. Wyatt rises and the brothers together cover the body with a slicker.
    Close-up of the slicker being drawn over James's head.

Medium shot of the three brothers, seen from above, so their faces are concealed by the rain, the darkness, and the broad brims of their hats.[7]

Dissolve to medium shot of an interior with a door in the center of the frame. Loud knocking is heard. The Mayor appears, wearing a bathrobe and carrying an oil lamp. He opens the door and Wyatt enters, still wearing his wet slicker.

WYATT: Mayor, is that marshalin' job still open?
MAYOR: It sure is.
WYATT: I'll take it.
MAYOR: It's yours. *(sets down lamp, turns back to Wyatt)*
WYATT: Providin' my brothers are my deputies.
MAYOR: When do you want to start?
WYATT: Now. *(They shake hands.)*

Wyatt starts to leave, then turns in the doorway.

WYATT: Who runs the gambling around here?
MAYOR: Doc Holliday, mostly.
WYATT: Who runs the cattle?
MAYOR: The Clantons. Old Man Clanton and his four sons.

Wyatt nods, turns, and closes the door behind him.

Fade in to the lobby of the Mansion House, Tombstone's hotel. The camera looks from the staircase toward the main entrance—double doors with glass panels covered with lace curtains. The doors are pushed open by two of the Clanton sons, both carrying shotguns. They stand at the doors and Old Man Clanton walks through, followed by Ike and Billy. They all wear slickers, wet with the rain that can be seen still falling in the street behind them. The five Clantons pause in the doorway as they react to something in front of them off-screen. Then Wyatt walks into the foreground; he has just come down the stairs from the Mayor's room. The camera looks over his shoulder at the Clantons.[8]

Close-up of Old Man Clanton, whose face suggests a mixture of surprise and cunning.

Close-up of Ike, impassive.

Close-up of Billy and Phin.

Close-up of Wyatt. The only sound is the rain falling heavily.

WYATT: Good evenin', Mr. Clanton.
CLANTON (CU): Good evenin'.
WYATT (CU): Fellow with the trail herd, remember.
CLANTON (MS *with Ike and Sam*): Oh, sure, I remember you.
WYATT (CU): You was right. I didn't get very far with 'em. They was rustled this evenin'.
CLANTON (*same* MS): That so. *(He smiles slightly.)* Well, that's too bad.

Long shot from behind Wyatt. Clanton moves into the hotel lobby.
Medium shot of the hotel's registration desk. Clanton begins to glance at the hotel's register, while Ike moves behind the desk to reach into one of the message boxes.

CLANTON (*over his shoulder*): Guess you'll be headin' for California, huh?

Medium shot of Wyatt turning in the doorway, flanked by the other three Clantons.

WYATT: No, I figured on stickin' around for awhile. Got myself a job.

Return to shot of Clanton and Ike.

CLANTON *(still not turning around)*: Cowpunchin'?
WYATT (MS): Marshalin'.
CLANTON *(MTS, now turning to look at Wyatt; Ike also looks up sharply)*:
   Marshalin'? In Tombstone? *(He moves to the end of the desk and begins to
   laugh mirthlessly.)* Well, good luck to you, Mr. . . . ?
WYATT *(off-screen)*: Earp. *(Clanton's expression changes; the name means
   something.)* Wyatt Earp.

*Return to medium shot of Wyatt with the Clanton boys in the doorway. He turns
and moves out of the hotel and out of the frame.*
   *Long shot of the porch from behind Wyatt as he slowly walks away from the
camera down the porch toward the corner as the scene fades out.*

---

*Fade in on long shot of open country with Wyatt dismounted, his horse next to
him. He is inserting a gravestone in a pile of rocks that serve to mark the
grave. He crosses to the far side of the grave and leans down. During this
entire scene, a solo guitar plays a slow ballad on the soundtrack.*
   *Medium shot across grave of Wyatt reaching down and shifting one of the
stones in order to prop the gravestone up more securely. The gravestone is
inscribed "*JAMES EARP / BORN / 1864 / DIED / 1882.*"*
   *Wyatt sits on the side of the grave, shifting some rocks with one hand while
staring at the grave marker.*

WYATT: Eighteen sixty-four—eighteen eighty-two. Eighteen years. Didn't get
   much of a chance, did you, James?

*A low-angle medium close-up of Wyatt from behind the gravestone. He con-
tinues to look at the marker and talk to James.*

WYATT: I wrote to Pa and Cory Sue. They're goin' to be all busted up over it.
   Cory Sue's young, but Pa—guess he'll never get over it. I'll be comin' out
   to see you regular, James. So will Morg and Virg. We're goin' to be around
   here for awhile. Can't tell—maybe when we leave this country, young kids
   like you will be able to grow up and live safe.

Wyatt pauses, then turns to get up.

Long shot of Wyatt as he mounts and rides toward the camera, turning in his saddle to look back at the grave. Fade out.

Fade in to long shot of the town of Tombstone seen from the road at the edge of town. A stagecoach enters the frame heading for Tombstone.[9]

Long shot of a gate and fence with the Tombstone jail in the background. Morgan stands at the gate, while Wyatt walks from the jail, a small adobe building, to join him.

Long shot from behind Morgan and Wyatt, showing the general activity of the road in front of them. People and wagons are moving about, with the mesas as a backdrop in the distance. A rider comes toward them from the open country, pulls up at the gate, and dismounts. It is Virgil.

Medium shot of the three brothers.

WYATT: Well, what did you find out?

VIRGIL: I followed their trail from the Clanton country to the river. They're moving cattle all right.

WYATT *(considering for a moment)*: Well, get yourself some sleep. *(He gives Virgil the keys to the jail.)* There's coffee on the stove, some beans. Morg's riding shotgun to Tucson.

Virgil heads off with his horse toward the building behind them.

MORGAN: Say, maybe I better ask around the banks while I'm down there, huh?
WYATT: Naw, they're too smart for that.

He and Morgan walk out of the frame, leaving only the jail in the background, with two Indians sitting in front of it.[10]

Dissolve to the Oriental Saloon. The camera looks down the length of a crowded bar from over the shoulders of two men at the upper end of the bar. When one moves away, we see the bartenders and the general activity of the drinkers.[11]
  Long shot of a card table at one side of the saloon. A seedy-looking older man in a top hat and dress coat is studying a poker hand. Next to him, looking down over his shoulder, stands Chihuahua, a dark-haired woman, dressed in a low-cut blouse and a Mexican skirt. She leans down and kisses the gambler. The camera follows her as she moves part way around the table, standing now between two players to the left of the gambler, one of whom is Wyatt. She puts her foot on the edge of the table very close to Wyatt, revealing a shapely leg. She never takes her eyes off him, but he puffs steadily on his cigar and leans forward to make a bet, ignoring her entirely.

VOICE *(off-screen)*: Hey, Chihuahua, sing us the one about the old blind mule.

Chihuahua catches a coin tossed from outside the frame, fingers it, looks at Earp sardonically, then walks to the rear where a group of musicians have been playing a lively dance tune. She whispers to one of them and they stop playing, then begin to play a slow ballad. The card game continues in the foreground. Chihuahua moves back to the card table, puts her hands on her hips provocatively, and begins to sing. She stands first on one side of Wyatt and then on the other. He continues to ignore her.

CHIHUAHUA: Ten thousand cattle gone astray,
            Left my range and wandered away,
            And the sons of guns, I'm here to say,

Medium close-up of Chihuahua.

Have left me dead broke, dead broke today.

Medium close-up of Wyatt; he folds his cards and tosses them back to the center of the table.

In gambling halls delaying,
Ten thousand cattle straying,

Medium shot of Chihuahua behind the table; she walks behind Wyatt back toward the gambler as she ends the song.

Ten thousand cattle straying.

As she is finishing the song, Wyatt finally looks up and they eye each other; he never changes expression and shows no particular interest in her. When he turns back to the table, she smiles scornfully, tosses the coin into his ashtray on the table, and saunters away.
Medium shot from inner side of the bar. Chihuahua pushes up to the bar through a crowd.

CHIHUAHUA *(to bartender, hesitantly)*: Hey, Mac, I hear Doc's comin' back
    tonight.
BARTENDER: Maybe he is, and maybe he ain't. I ain't heard.
CHIHUAHUA (CU): Well, do you know where he's been.
BARTENDER: Tucson . . . over the border. Who knows where Doc goes.

Medium shot out over bartender's shoulder. Chihuahua looks at him, turns away slowly, and starts to move back into the main part of the saloon.
Long shot of card table and back area of saloon. Chihuahua crosses to window in back, looks out, then approaches the card table to stand behind Wyatt on his left. While she moves, Wyatt is speaking.

WYATT: I love poker. Yes sir, I really love poker. Every hand a different prob-
    lem. I gotta do a little figurin' here. What would I do if I was in your boots,
    Mr. Gambler?

Medium close-up of Chihuahua looking directly to her left.

Reverse close-up of the gambler looking to his right.
Return to the shot of Chihuahua, now raising three fingers.
Medium shot of Wyatt hunched over his cards, half turned in his seat toward the gambler.

WYATT *(quizzically)*: You drew three cards, an' I stood pat, and yet you raised me.

Wyatt glances toward the gambler.
   Close-up of gambler suddenly snapping his attention back from Chihuahua to the cards in his hand.
   Medium shot of Wyatt. He tilts his chair back so that he is leaning into Chihuahua.

WYATT: Now the question is, what should I do? *(He looks up at Chihuahua for a long moment.)*

Long shot of the table and back of saloon with Wyatt at center of frame. He gets up.

WYATT: Yeah, mighty interesting game, poker. *(He tosses his cards onto the table.)* Game of chance. *(As he turns away from the table, he reaches out quickly behind him, grabs Chihuahua by the arm, and pulls her after him, leaving the frame at the left.)*

Long shot outside the side door of the saloon. Wyatt appears from the right, still pulling Chihuahua after him. In semidarkness, he swings her around so that she is standing in front of a horse trough, facing him. They are in profile to the camera.

WYATT: Listen, miss. I admire poker, but you're increasin' the odds. If I catch you doin' that again, I'll run you back to the Apache reservation where you belong.
CHIHUAHUA *(interrupting)*: Listen, Mr. Tin Star Marshal, this is Doc Holliday's town, and when he comes back . . . *(She slaps Wyatt across the face.)*

Wyatt takes her by the shoulders and pushes her back and down into the watering trough, so that she sits half-submerged, as if in a bathtub. Then he turns and leaves the frame. Chihuahua stands up, dripping and spluttering, and begins to wring out her shawl.

Long shot across card table looking into main part of saloon. Camera pans with Wyatt as he crosses to his seat, holding his hat in one hand and brushing it with the other.

WYATT *(to the table)*: Sorry, gents, but I don't like eight-handed poker games.
GAMBLER: Oh, Mr. Marshal, you don't think that I had . . .
WYATT *(putting on his hat and sitting down)*: No, no.

Medium shot of Wyatt and player on his left.

WYATT: Well, where were we.
CARD PLAYER: He just raised you, Marshal.
WYATT *(looking to his right toward the gambler)*: Oh, yeah. *(slowly)* Well, seeing as you know I got three of a kind *(folds his cards)* guess I'll . . . *(tosses the cards in)*

Camera moves over and down so that only Wyatt and the card table in front of him are seen. The gambler's hands begin to pull in the chips, then stop. Wyatt looks from the table toward the gambler, then out across the table into the room.

Long shot from behind the bar as a striking figure dressed in black carrying a saddlebag crosses the saloon and comes up to the bar. He tosses his bag onto the bar, while keeping his eyes focused on the interior of the saloon ahead of him. Camera pans to include bartender who leans forward toward the man in black.

BARTENDER: Hiya, Doc.

Doc Holliday, still staring out into the saloon, pats the bartender's arm.
Medium shot of Doc, staring directly out into the room.

BARTENDER *(off-screen)*: Good trip?

Doc reacts to something he sees; his face tightens with displeasure.
Medium shot of Wyatt at card table, with the profile of the gambler in the

foreground. The gambler concentrates on stacking up the chips, obviously not wanting to look up. Earp still looks out in Holliday's direction with some curiosity.

CARD PLAYER *(off-screen)*: Doc Holliday.
WYATT *(leaning back in his chair, to gambler)*: Nice-lookin' fella.

The gambler does not reply, but just continues stacking chips. Then he looks furtively out into the room.
  Medium shot of Holliday, who begins to move forward and out of frame.

BARTENDER *(off-screen)*: Doc, don't lets have any trouble now.

Long shot from behind the gambler of Doc advancing down the length of the bar toward the card table. As he reaches the gambler, Doc, with a quick swing of his arm, knocks the gambler's top hat off his head. The music stops abruptly.
  Medium shot of Doc looking down at gambler.[12]

DOC: I told you to get out of town and stay out.

Long shot of Holliday and the card table from a viewpoint near the bar. The gambler gets up.

GAMBLER: Aw, Doc, I'll cut you in on the game.
DOC: I told you to get out of town.
GAMBLER *(straightens his coat, picks up his hat, turns to table)*: Check me in, will ya? *(He starts to go around Doc to head down the aisle toward the front door. Doc catches his arm.)*
DOC *(after a pause)*: That door's for ladies and gentlemen.

Camera pans with gambler as he heads out the side door, the one that Wyatt and Chihuahua had used moments earlier.
  Medium shot from the bar side of the card table.
  Doc turns and stands behind the gambler's empty chair.

DOC: Go on with your game, gentlemen.

Long shot from behind the card table and the empty seat as Doc walks back up the length of the bar, disappearing in the haze of smoke that obscures the far end of the room. All the card players turn to watch him go; since Wyatt is seated facing out into the room, he does not move at all. After a pause, the players begin turning back to the table.

CARD PLAYER: Well, you can cash me in. It's getting late. I'll see you all later.

He gets up; a second player gets up too.
Medium shot of Wyatt at the table, with the hands of the player next to him visible stacking the chips back in their box.

WYATT: It sure is a hard town for a fella to have a quiet game of poker in.

He gets up, takes his hat off, rakes the chips in front of him into the hat, puts the hat back on his head, turns, and leaves the frame.
Long shot from behind the table; the bar is completely deserted now, as everybody has moved back away from it. Only the figure of Doc is visible through the haze, leaning on the bar near its far end, staring straight ahead at the wall. Wyatt very slowly walks the length of the bar.
Medium shot with Doc in foreground as Wyatt advances toward him. Doc does not turn, but he looks tense, expectant. Wyatt passes behind him, coming around to stand at the corner of the bar, so that he now faces Doc while we see only Wyatt's back.

WYATT: Howdy.
DOC: Good evening.
WYATT: I'm . . .
DOC *(interrupting)*: Wyatt Earp. I know. I know all about you and your reason for being here.

Reverse shot toward Wyatt.

WYATT: I've heard a lot about you too, Doc. You've left your mark around in Deadwood, Denver, and places. In fact a man could almost follow your trail, going from graveyard to graveyard.
DOC (CU): There's one here, too. Biggest graveyard west of the Rockies. Marshals and I usually get along much better when we understand that right away.

WYATT (CU): Get your meanin', Doc.
DOC (CU): Good. Have a drink.
WYATT (CU): Thanks. Believe I will.

Long shot behind and between the two men toward the bartender, who is half-way down the bar.

DOC: Mac, a glass of champagne for the Marshal.
WYATT: Make it whiskey.
DOC: You're my guest, Marshal. *(As the bartender slides a whiskey glass up the bar to Wyatt, Doc, without taking his eyes off Wyatt, blocks the glass with his hand and sends it sliding back.)* Champagne. *(A pause. The bartender freezes in place.)*
WYATT: Champagne it is, Mac.

Medium shot of the saloon musicians grouped at the other end of the bar. Camera pans as they move to the stand and begin to play "Camptown Races" at a lively tempo.

Medium shot of Doc and Wyatt with champagne glasses in hand. They touch glasses and drink. Doc watches Wyatt carefully; Earp pulls a face at the taste of champagne and stares down unhappily at his glass.

Long shot from behind the two men, looking down the bar. The bar is empty for some distance down from Doc.

DOC: Plan on staying here long?
WYATT: A while.
DOC: Until you catch the rustlers who killed your brother?
WYATT: That's the general idea.
DOC: What's the . . . specific idea?
WYATT: I don't follow you quite.
DOC: You haven't taken it into your head to deliver us from all evil?

Medium shot of Wyatt and Doc from behind the bar.

WYATT: I hadn't thought of it quite like that, but it ain't a bad idea. It's what I'm gettin' paid for.
DOC: Let's get down to cases, Marshal. I, for instance. *(Moves his hands close to the edge of the bar.)* How would you handle me if I took a notion to break the law.

Medium shot of Wyatt from behind Doc.

WYATT *(more firmly)*: You already have.
DOC: For example?
WYATT: Runnin' that tinhorn out of town. That's none of your business.

Doc takes a drink of champagne. He puts his hands back on the edge of the bar.

DOC: I see we're in opposite camps, Marshal. Draw! *(He pulls a gun and holds it on Wyatt. The saloon becomes silent.)*

Earp begins to smile; he lifts the side of his vest to reveal only his shirt.

WYATT: Can't.
DOC: We can take care of that easily enough.

Long shot down the bar. Holliday turns toward the bartender.

DOC: Mac!

As the bartender reaches under the counter, Morgan Earp, who is now stand-ing midway down the bar, but with no one else between him and Doc, takes out his gun and slides it up to Wyatt.

WYATT *(picking up the gun and examining it)*: My brother Morg's gun.

He slides the gun back down the bar to Morgan. Doc turns to look at Morgan, who picks the gun up, plays with it for a moment, then puts it back in his holster.
    Medium two shot of Doc and Wyatt. Doc is still looking down the bar toward Morgan. Slowly he turns back toward Wyatt, away from the camera. He puts his gun away and resumes his old stance, leaning against the bar.

WYATT: The big one, that's Morg. The other one, that good-lookin' fella, that's my brother Virg. This is Doc Holliday, fellas. *(Doc looks down the bar again, with a half smile.)*

Medium shot of Morgan, turned to face up the bar, with Virgil half hidden behind him.

MORGAN: Hiya, Doc.
VIRGIL: Howdy.

Medium shot of Doc and Wyatt.

DOC *(with forced brightness)*: Howdy. *(He looks back at Wyatt, then toward Morgan.)* Have a drink.[13]

Long shot down the bar. Music strikes up, and all the patrons, who have moved back away from the bar since Wyatt first went up to Doc, now rush forward. The bartender approaches with glasses and a cut glass decanter as Morg and Virg move up to join the other two men.

MORGAN: Don't mind if I do, Doc.

DOC: Join us, Mac.

BARTENDER: Yes, thanks. *(He gets another glass.)*

DOC: Gentlemen. *(He raises his glass, turns toward Morgan.)* Your health.

WYATT: Your health, Doc. *(Doc turns back, suspecting irony, then smiles.)*

They all drink, and Doc begins to cough violently. He takes out a white hand-kerchief to cover the cough until it subsides, then he gulps down the rest of his drink. The Earps stare at Doc; the bartender shakes his head in sympathetic warning to Doc.

Long shot of front entrance of saloon seen from inside. Old Dad comes in carrying valises. He holds the door open so that a dandyish gentleman, Granville Thorndyke, may make a grand entrance. Cheers go up as the man walks in, comes to a dramatic stop, and acknowledges the crowd by raising his top hat and saying, in highly cultivated tones, "Thank you." He seems totally out of place in the saloon. The man pauses a moment and then walks with great self-assurance up to where Doc and Wyatt are standing. He raps on the bar sharply with his cane.

THORNDYKE: Come, come, my good man. Let me have service or I'll take my patronage elsewhere. *(He barely pays attention to the Earps and Doc, stares down at the floor for a moment, and motions to Wyatt brusquely with his hand.)* Your foot, sir.

Wyatt moves and Thorndyke puts his foot up on the bar rail. He spots Wyatt's champagne glass, still half full, on the bar, drinks it down, pronounces "Champagne," then turns and, as camera pans, sits down at a nearby table where Old Dad is already seated. Dad begins to beat vehemently on the table for service.

Medium shot of Wyatt and Doc at the bar.

WYATT *(leaning over to Doc so that he can be heard above the noise)*: The actor in tonight's show.

DOC *(musing)*: Shakespeare in Tombstone.

Medium shot of Thorndyke's table. Dad is still pounding on the table.

BARTENDER *(off-screen)*: Coming right up, Mr. Shakespeare.

Return to medium shot of Wyatt and Doc.

DOC: It's a long time since I heard Shakespeare. How would you like to join me tonight, Marshal?

WYATT: Yeah, fine. Better see that he gets to the theatre or there won't be any show. *(He turns back to the bar, puts his drink down, bends his head to take off his hat, and dumps the chips he has been carrying in it on the bar. He pushes them toward the bartender.)* Mac, cash in for me, will ya.

Long shot of Thorndyke's table. Wyatt walks around it and stands behind the actor and Dad.

WYATT: Dad, take Mr. Thorndyke over to the Birdcage.

THORNDYKE *(huffily)*: Birdcage? You're incarcerating me in a birdcage, sir? *(He is helped up by Wyatt, joined by Virgil, but he has trouble keeping his balance. Clearly, he is quite drunk.)*

WYATT: That's the name of the theater.

THORNDYKE: The theater? *(recollecting)* The show! Good heavens! The show must go on. Lead on!

He points to Dad to lead the way, then follows him through the swinging doors. Wyatt and Virgil leave frame left, moving back toward the bar. Before the doors have stopped swinging, Thorndyke reappears, throws his arms out, announces "Drinks on the house!", turns, and disappears again. Fade out.

Fade in to a poster announcing "The Convict's Oath" starring Granville Thorndyke and Company.

Long shot of the interior of the Birdcage Theater seen from the back, looking toward the lighted stage over the heads of the audience. The theater is packed with people.

Long shot of two boxes next to the stage filled with the girls from the dance hall. They are all laughing and reaching down to a cluster of men who are standing just below the boxes, reaching up to them.

Low angle shot in front of Mexican woman who moves through the crowd selling tamales.

Medium long shot of another box where Doc and Wyatt are sitting alone. Chihuahua comes through a curtain at the back, leans over Doc, and lifting his hat, kisses him. As she straightens up, she becomes aware of Wyatt and glares at him.

DOC *(getting up, as does Wyatt)*: May I present my friend, Wyatt Earp.
CHIHUAHUA: Him, a friend!
DOC: He, not him.
CHIHUAHUA: Well, he or him. He ain't no friend of mine. *(She sits down next to Doc. The men sit down.)*
WYATT: What she's tryin' to say, Doc, is that we've met before. Sorta found ourselves together in an eight-handed poker game.

Medium long shot of the stage. A trumpeter standing at the side of the stage sounds a call. The theater owner comes from behind the curtain, holding his top hat in his hand.

THEATER OWNER *(clearing his throat and then bellowing)*: Laa-deez . . .

Medium shot of the dance-hall girls cheering wildly.

THEATER OWNER *(in medium shot, showing only the stage)*: . . . and gentlemen.

Long shot of stage and audience, as men cheer wildly.

THEATER OWNER: Owing to circumstances that I had nothing to do with, the show "The Convict's Oath" will not appear tonight. *(Loud indignation; the owner holds up his hand for quiet; medium low angle shot of owner on the stage.)* But, as if I didn't already have enough trouble, that eminent actor, that sterling tragedian, Mr. Granville . . . *(He begins to scratch his head; he has forgotten the name.)*

Return to long shot that includes the audience.

AUDIENCE: Thorndyke!!
THEATER OWNER: . . . has completely disappeared. *(Great uproar from the audience.)*

Long shot looking across stage from Doc's box, which is closest to the stage.

The owner tries to cross to the box, as members of the audience try to pull him down into the crowd.

Long shot of Doc's box as seen from just above the heads of the audience. The owner is trying to crawl head first into the box, with the audience pulling him back. Chihuahua is beating the manager on the head with Doc's hat. Wyatt stands up and the owner gets into the box and hides behind him. A long wooden bench is being passed over the heads of the audience until it is held directly in front of the box. Old Dad comes into the box from the back during the melee and whispers into Wyatt's ear.

WYATT *(to crowd)*: Wait a minute. What are ya acting so mad about?

Medium shot of crowd of men holding up the wooden bench.

MAN IN CROWD: Why, this is the fourth time this year this has happened, Marshal.
SECOND MAN: Bird imitators, bird imitators, that's all we get.

Long shot of Doc's box.

THEATER OWNER *(from behind Wyatt)*: Gentlemen, I can explain that.
WYATT *(cutting in)*: Well, what are ya fixin' to do about it?

Return to medium shot of crowd.

MAN IN CROWD: Look, Marshal, be reasonable. All we want to do is to ride him around town a couple of times on the rail.

Long shot of the box again.

WYATT: Well, that sounds reasonable enough to me. *(He puts his arm around the owner's shoulder and pushes him gently in the direction of the crowd; the owner starts to slide down toward the floor of the box. Then as the uproar begins again . . .)* Wait a minute, wait a minute. I've got a better idea. Just give me fifteen minutes and I think I can find this Mr. . . . (shouts of "Thorndyke") I'll bring him back in. Now sit down and take your seats again and have another beer. *(He exits frame, leaving the box.)*[14]

Dissolve to long shot of another saloon. Thorndyke, in black tights and cape, is standing on a table. In front of him is Ike Clanton, the other brothers are in the background.

IKE *(sounding mean)*: Look, Yorick, can't you give us nothin' but them poems.
THORNDYKE *(loftily)*: I have a very large repertoire, sir.
IKE: Great. All right, Yorick, go ahead. Shoot.

Ike goes over to join two of his brothers leaning against the bar. Phin, the third, is seated at a table behind Thorndyke. Thorndyke has a bottle in his hand; he takes a long swig from it.
    A long shot of many Mexicans standing in the saloon watching.
    Return to previous long shot of Thorndyke and the Clantons. Thorndyke puts the bottle down on the table; as he prepares himself to recite, Sam shoots the bottle to pieces, and all of the Clantons laugh uproariously. Thorndyke again prepares himself and, turning away from the Clantons, speaks to off-screen left.

THORNDYKE: Minstrel, pray help me.

Medium shot of piano player at upright who begins to play softly.
    Medium shot from behind Wyatt and Doc just outside the saloon door. Wyatt starts to enter, but Doc stops him.

DOC: Wait. I want to hear this.

Return to long shot of Thorndyke on the table. He bows with great formality in the direction of the piano player, says "Thank you," and then begins to recite, looking not at the Clantons, but up and out into the middle distance.

THORNDYKE: To be or not to be—

Low-angle medium close-up of Thorndyke.

                              that is the question;
                 Whether 'tis nobler in the mind to suffer
                 The slings and arrows of outrageous fortune,
                 Or to take arms against a sea of troubles,

And by opposing end them?

Long shot of Doc followed by Wyatt moving forward through the group of Mexicans in the saloon; when Doc reaches the front of the group, he stops, puts one leg up on the seat of a chair and leans forward, engrossed in what he is hearing; Thorndyke's voice continues off-screen during the shot.

To die, to sleep—
No more; and by a sleep to say we end
The heart-ache

Return to previous close-up of Thorndyke.

and the thousand natural shocks
That flesh is heir to. 'Tis a consummation
Devoutly to be wish'd. To die,

Medium long shot of Doc, with Wyatt behind him.

to sleep;
To sleep, perchance to dream.

Return to Thorndyke close-up.

Ay, there's the rub;
For in that sleep of death what dreams may come
When we have shuffled off this mortal coil

IKE *(off-screen)*: That's enough. That's enough.

Long shot of the three Clantons leaning against the bar. Ike, who is standing farthest back, takes a drink and then smashes his glass on the floor. He walks forward past his brothers toward the camera.

IKE: You don't know nothin' but them poems. You can't sing. Maybe you can dance.
DOC *(off-screen)*: Leave him alone.

All three brothers whirl toward the camera. Ike, glaring, is furious.
  Return to previous shot of Doc and Wyatt.

DOC: Please go on, Mr. Thorndyke.

Long shot from behind Doc and Wyatt of Thorndyke and the Clantons.

THORNDYKE: Thank you, sir.
            Must give us pause.

Medium shot from below Thorndyke, with Ike Clanton in the foreground, Sam standing behind him.

                    There's the respect
            That makes calamity of so long life;
            For who would bear the whips and scorns of time,

Medium close-up of Thorndyke.

            The law's delay
            The insolence of office, and the spurns
            That patient merit of th' unworthy takes,
            When he himself might his quietus make

Thorndyke slowly raises a dagger and stares at it.

            With a bare bodkin? Who would fardels bear,
            To grunt and sweat under a weary life . . . life . . .

Thorndyke looks blank; he cannot remember the lines. He drops his head, and covers his face with the hand holding the dagger. The dagger falls out of his hand. He looks up again toward Doc.

            Please help me, sir.
DOC (CU): But that the dread of something after death . . .

Repeat of the medium shot of Thorndyke with the Clantons.

THORNDYKE: Would you carry on? I'm afraid . . . *(apologetically)* It's been so long.

Close-up of Wyatt, looking over toward Doc.

DOC (CU): The undiscovered country, from whose bourn
                            No traveller returns

Return to close-up of Wyatt, still looking toward Doc.

                            puzzles the will,
                 And makes us rather bear those ills we have

Return to close-up of Doc.

                 Than fly to others that we know not of?
                 Thus conscience does make cowards of us all . . .

Doc begins coughing.
   Close-up of Wyatt watching him.
   Close-up of Doc with his face bent down into his handkerchief.
   Return to the close-up of Wyatt as Doc continues coughing.
   Long shot of the saloon from behind Doc and Wyatt. Doc turns, still cough-ing violently, and heads toward the door of the saloon.
   Medium shot outside the saloon doors as Doc pushes through them and leaves frame on the left.
   Long shot from behind Wyatt. Camera pans slightly to take in the four Clantons, all now standing and facing Wyatt, as well as Thorndyke, who is still on the table. After a pause, Wyatt sets aside a chair and moves slowly toward Thorndyke.

WYATT: They're waiting for you at the theater, Mr. Thorndyke.

He helps Thorndyke down from the table.

THORNDYKE: Thank you, sir. Shakespeare was not meant for taverns *(he looks meaningfully at Ike)*, nor for tavern louts.

IKE *(stepping in)*: Yorick stays here. *(He grabs Thorndyke to pull him over, but Wyatt hits Ike over the head with his gun barrel. Ike falls.)*

Medium shot from behind Wyatt of Phin drawing his gun. Wyatt fires and Phin falls backward, his gun flying behind him.
  Medium shot of Billy and Sam Clanton slowly raising their hands.
  Medium shot of Old Man Clanton coming through a half-open door at the back of the saloon. Behind him, women can be seen moving about and excited women's voices can be heard.

WOMAN'S VOICE: Qué pasa! Qué pasa! Parece que hay banditos!

Clanton looks first down toward the floor where Phin must be lying, then looks up and sees Wyatt; his face hardens.
  Long shot from the other end of the saloon. Clanton comes forward until he reaches the spot where Wyatt stands on one side, with his gun still pointed at Billy and Sam, Ike sitting on the floor between his brothers.

CLANTON *(quietly)*: My apologies, Marshal. Ike and Phin have had a little whiskey.
WYATT *(putting his gun away)*: Sure, I figure they was just havin' themselves a little fun. *(He turns and starts out of the saloon, along with Thorndyke.)* Come on, Mr. Thorndyke, I'll take you to the theater. *(They both exit in the foreground.)*[15]

Clanton stands looking after Wyatt, then takes his whip and begins beating the three sons at the bar. They all cower away from him, holding their arms up for cover and crying "Stop, Pa, stop."
  After six or seven blows, Clanton stands back from them.

CLANTON *(starting to walk out of the saloon)*: When ya pull a gun, kill a man.
SON'S VOICE *(weakly)*: Yes, Pa.

Clanton walks out of frame in foreground and scene fades out.[16]

―――――――――

Fade in on long establishing shot of road into Tombstone. The town seems

diminished by the flat, uninhabited space around it and by the giant mesas in the background.

Long shot from porch of Mansion House. Two women who work at the hotel stand on the porch watching the stagecoach approaching on a road running parallel to the road in front of the hotel. Wyatt is sitting in a chair at the front edge of the porch. As the three watch, the stage loops around and pulls up in front of the hotel.

Low-angle medium shot from the side of the stagecoach up at the driver and his relief man on the top.

DRIVER: All out for breakfast! All out for breakfast!

Long shot from the sidewalk corner of the coach and the sidewalk in front of the Mansion House. The hotel clerk has opened the coach door and passengers are emerging and walking in to the Mansion House.

PASSENGER'S VOICE: How are you this mornin', Earp?
WYATT: Fine.

After this exchange one passenger stops at the edge of the hotel veranda. Earp is sitting with his chair tilted back and one foot propped up against a front post of the veranda. He does not appear to be looking at the man standing near him.[17]

WYATT: How are things in Deadwood, Mr. Gambler?

Medium shot of the gambler and Wyatt.

GAMBLER: All right, I guess.
WYATT: Brother with you?
GAMBLER: No.
WYATT *(still not looking at him)*: Get yourself some flapjacks. The stage is
   leaving in thirty minutes. *(pause, then with emphasis)* See you're on it.

Gambler passes on into the hotel, leaving Wyatt still motionless.
   *Medium shot of side of stagecoach as hotel clerk helps Clementine Carter
out. The only woman passenger, she is young and attractive. A slow version of
"My Darling Clementine" is played on the soundtrack.*

CLEMENTINE: *(to clerk)*: Thank you. *(She stands in the road and looks
   around at her surroundings.)*

Medium shot of Wyatt from the side. He stands up and pushes his hat back.

CLERK *(off-screen)*: I'll prepare a room for you.

*Long shot from behind Wyatt on the porch. The clerk leaves Clementine and
rushes into the hotel. She looks around her, and then advances to the porch,
but instead of entering the hotel, she turns and stands looking out into the road.*

WYATT: Can I help you, ma'am? Old Dad's usually here to take care of the
   . . . *(He walks a few steps past her down the sidewalk and turns back.)* Is
   that your duffle up there?
CLEMENTINE: Yes.

*Camera pans with Wyatt as he walks out to the stage and climbs up to where
the baggage is stowed on the roof.*

Medium long shot from inside hotel dining room, looking through the room to the door and vestibule of the hotel. At a center table facing the camera sits Morgan.

MORGAN *(to waitress)*: Alice, just give me a stack of buckwheat cakes with plenty of molasses and a steak, blood rare, and a couple o' hunks of bacon, if you got some, and a big pot of . . . *(He pauses, catching sight of Clementine, who has just come in the door of the hotel, followed by Wyatt, who is carrying her bags.)* . . . coffee.

Morgan turns around in his chair to watch her as she goes to the hotel desk in the background.
    Long shot of hotel desk with clerk behind it as Clementine approaches from foreground, with Wyatt still behind her.

CLEMENTINE: I'm looking for Dr. John Holliday.

Medium shot of Wyatt holding her bags.

WYATT: You mean Doc Holliday?

Medium shot of Clementine from behind the hotel desk.

CLEMENTINE: I imagine so.
CLERK: Oh, Doc Holliday. Why, he rode out of town about three o'clock this morning heading south. I don't know when he'll be back, ma'am.

Camera pans over to include Wyatt, who walks into the frame.

WYATT: He'll most likely be back suppertime. Maybe you'd like to have some breakfast, freshen up a bit.
CLEMENTINE: I would like some coffee.
WYATT *(to clerk)*: Have you got a room for Miss . . .
CLEMENTINE: Carter. Clementine Carter.

Clerk presents her with the hotel register and she signs it.
    Medium shot of Morgan and Virgil in the dining room, still staring out toward the hotel desk.

Medium shot of Clementine and Wyatt, seen from behind the hotel desk. She finishes signing the register, thanks the clerk, and leaves the frame on the right.

WYATT *(glancing down at the register)*: See if Josephina can't get a couple of buckets of hot water . . . so she can take a bath.
CLERK: Yes, Marshal.

Long shot of upstairs hotel corridor. Clementine, followed by Wyatt with the bags, comes up the stairs at the far end. They walk down the corridor toward the camera.

WYATT: That's Doc's room. You're right across the hall from him.
CLEMENTINE: John's room? *(As Wyatt unlocks her door on the right, she pushes open the door opposite.)*[18]

Long shot from inside Doc's room, looking toward the door. Clementine enters, looking around. She notices a picture on the wall.

CLEMENTINE: Oh, that's John with a moustache.

Camera pans with her as she walks around the room, stops at the far wall to look at a framed diploma, and then notices a doctor's bag on the table beneath it.

CLEMENTINE: *(turning back to Wyatt)*: He is a good surgeon, isn't he.
WYATT *(not advancing beyond the door frame)*: I wouldn't know, ma'am.

Return to previous shot. Clementine turns and starts to leave the room.
   Return to medium shot of Wyatt in the doorway. Clementine enters the frame from the right, then pauses to look down at some object on the bureau.

WYATT: That's a nice picture of you.

Close-up of elaborately framed photograph of Clementine in a nurse's uniform.
   Medium shot of Clementine moving into doorway, as Wyatt, back in the corridor, opens the door across the way. She turns and looks back into Holliday's room for a moment, then closes the door as the scene fades out.

Fade in to long establishing shot looking across street toward the Mansion

House where the stagecoach is now being readied for its departure. A group of women with parasols cross the street to join a large crowd on the porch in front of the hotel. The horses are brought around and attached to the coach.

VOICE IN CROWD: All right, folks. All together, now.
CROWD: Hip-hip-hooray!

Medium shot of Mayor and Thorndyke in the center of the crowd.

MAYOR: The town of Tombstone is most grateful to you for a wonderful performance.
THORNDYKE: Mr. Mayor, I am most touched by your tribute.
BARBER *(pushing his way in)*: Have one of my cards.
THORNDYKE *(taking it as homage)*: Thank you very much, sir.

The Mayor steps aside and is replaced by the hotel clerk.

CLERK: Sorry you're leaving, Mr. Thorndyke. *(in lower voice)* Here's your bill.
THORNDYKE *(momentarily nonplussed)*: The bill. *(Then with a great flourish he autographs it, folds it, and gives it back to the clerk with a fervent "Thank you." The clerk looks baffled as Thorndyke exits frame on right.)*

Long shot of side of stagecoach away from the hotel. Thorndyke appears from rear of stage, ready to embark. As he stores his bag, he looks behind him to see Old Dad standing in the road.
    Thorndyke turns to face Old Dad.

THORNDYKE: Great souls by instinct to each other turn,
             Demand allegiance, and in friendship burn.*

He extends both hands and takes each of Old Dad's hands.

             Good night, sweet prince.

Close-up of Old Dad looking touched and abashed.

*Adapted from Joseph Addison, *The Campaign* (1705), ll. 101–102.

*Return to previous shot. Thorndyke turns and climbs up on the stage next to
the driver. Above him in the background, on the upper veranda of the Mansion
House, two cleaning women look down.*

CLEANING WOMAN: Goodbye, Mistah Actor!
THORNDYKE *(waving his hat)*: Parting is such sweet sorrow!

*The driver cracks his whip and the stage pulls out of the frame.
    Long shot of road into town with stage heading away from town and toward
the camera.*

Close-up of Chihuahua with a guitar.[19]
    *Long shot from back of saloon. Clementine moves through the crowd toward
the back where Chihuahua is sitting and playing. She sits down at an empty
table nearest to the music stand.
    Close-up of Clementine. She is looking toward Chihuahua and she smiles
at her.
    Close-up of Chihuahua. She makes no response to Clementine's expression.
    Long shot of back of the saloon, including both Clementine and Chihuahua.
The bartender comes over and wipes the table.*

BARTENDER: Would ya like a glass of beer, ma'am?
CLEMENTINE: No, thank you. *(She stands up.)* I'm looking for Dr. John Holli-
    day. *(Medium shot of Clementine and bartender.)*
BARTENDER: Who?
CLEMENTINE: Dr. John Holliday.

*Close-up of Chihuahua, now very interested.
    Return to long shot of back of saloon.*

BARTENDER: Oh. *(doubtfully)* Well, I'll see if I can find him for you, ma'am.
    (He heads toward the kitchen door in the background.)
CLEMENTINE: *(sitting down again)*: Thank you.

*Close-up of Chihuahua looking toward Clementine.
    Long shot from behind Chihuahua looking across the music stand
toward Clementine's table. The bartender reappears in frame.*

BARTENDER: Go right in, ma'am.
CLEMENTINE: Thank you. *(She gets up and exits frame on the right.)*

Long shot across a dining table in the kitchen toward the door to the saloon. Wyatt and Doc are seated at the table. Clementine comes through the door, and Doc rises.
  Close-up of Doc, looking shocked.
  Close-up of Clementine, smiling, expectant. Her smile begins to fade.

CLEMENTINE: Hello, John.
DOC (CU): Clem!

Long shot from behind the table. Clementine comes forward and presses Doc's hands. Wyatt gets up from the table and starts to leave.

DOC *(to Clementine)*: I'd like you to meet a friend of mine. Wyatt Earp. Miss Clementine Carter.

CLEMENTINE: We've met, John. Good evening, Mr. Earp. *(She shakes hands.)*
WYATT: Howdy, ma'am. I'll see you both later. *(He goes out the kitchen door.)*

Long shot of Wyatt coming out of the kitchen into the saloon. He walks toward the bar, where Morgan is standing.

WYATT: Let's eat.
MORGAN: What are you up to?

They move out of the frame, leaving Chihuahua seated on the music stand. Behind her only a low partition separates the stand from the kitchen in back. She gets up and goes over to the partition.
   Medium shot of the partition, seen from the kitchen side, with Chihuahua's face appearing over the top.
   Long shot from back of kitchen, looking across the kitchen table. Clementine and Doc sit next to each other (at right angles).

CLEMENTINE: It's wonderful to see you again, John.

Medium shot of Clementine and Doc. Doc does not look at her.

CLEMENTINE: You are pleased that I came? *(A pause; Doc is silent.)* My coming has made you unhappy.
DOC: It was ill-advised.
CLEMENTINE: Any less ill-advised than the way you left Boston?
DOC *(turning to her)*: How'd you know I was here?
CLEMENTINE (CU): I didn't. Finding you hasn't been easy. From cowcamp to cowcamp, (CU *Doc*) from one mining town to another. (CU *Clementine*) I should think that if nothing more you'd be at least flattered to have a girl chase you.

Medium shot of Clementine and Doc.

DOC: Look, Clem, you've got to get out of here.
CLEMENTINE: But I'm not.
DOC: This is no place for your kind of person.

CLEMENTINE: What kind of a person am I, John?
DOC (CU): Please go back home, Clem. Back where you belong. Forget
   the . . . *(He begins to cough.)*

Long shot of the table looking toward the back door. Doc, still coughing, gets
up and goes out that door.
   Clementine gets up and follows.
   Medium shot of the back door from the outside, as Clementine opens it. She
stands in the doorway with the chef behind her.
   Medium shot of Doc seen from the back; he is kneeling, and leaning over the
rail to the porch, still coughing.
   Return to shot of Clementine and François, the chef.

CLEMENTINE: Does this happen to John frequently?
FRANÇOIS: Oui, mademoiselle. Each time is worse.

Clementine advances out of frame.
   Medium shot of Doc, still on his knees with his back to the camera. Clemen-
tine enters right and stands beside him, looking down at him.

CLEMENTINE: You're ill, John. So that's the reason you left.
DOC: That has nothing to do with it.
CLEMENTINE: Foolish, foolish, John. As if that would have mattered.
DOC: I tell you, Clem, the condition of my health has nothing to do with it.
CLEMENTINE: I don't believe you, John.

Doc turns to look at her, then stands to face her.

DOC: Then I'll give you the truth. The man you once knew is no more. There's
   not a vestige of him left. Nothing. Come, I'll take you back to the hotel.[20]

Close-up of Doc and Clementine facing each other.

CLEMENTINE: Please, John. You can't send me away like this. You can't run
   away from me any more than you can run away from yourself. Now I know
   why you don't care whether you live or die. Why you tried to get yourself

killed. Oh, I've heard all about you, John, and you're wrong, so wrong. You've no right to destroy yourself. You have a world of friends back home who love you, John, and I love you.

Medium shot of Clementine and Doc facing each other.

DOC: There's a stage leaving in the morning for the East. Take it. If you don't, I'm moving on.
CLEMENTINE *(after a pause)*: Very well, John. I'll go.

She turns, he takes her arm, and they move out of frame on the right.

———————

Dissolve to medium shot from inside Doc's room.[21] *Doc enters and camera pans with him as he crosses the room to the far wall where his framed diplomas hang. The only light comes through the window from the street. Doc sits at the foot of his bed, looking at his diplomas in the darkness. He pours himself a drink from a bottle that stands on the desk below the diplomas and gulps the drink down.*
Medium shot from behind Doc. His face is reflected in the covering glass over the lower diploma.

DOC *(with self-disgust)*: Doctor John Holliday!

He throws the whiskey glass at the diploma, shattering the covering glass and with it his reflection.

———————

Dissolve to long shot toward door of the saloon from point behind a table where the Earps are eating. Doc comes through the doors, sees Wyatt, and stops.

DOC: From where I'm standing, Earp, that tin badge you're wearing doesn't give you the right to stick your nose into my personal affairs.
WYATT *(easily)*: What's eatin' ya, Doc?
DOC: Why didn't you tell me Miss Carter was here?

Reverse shot of table from behind Doc.

WYATT: She told you why. She wanted to surprise you.

Reverse shot from behind table. Doc walks on into the saloon.
    Long shot down the saloon. Doc walks up to the bar. In background Chihuahua, wearing a huge Mexican sombrero, is talking to musicians on the stand. As the bartender approaches him, Doc picks up a glass on the bar, looks at it, and pushes it savagely up the bar and out of frame. Sound of glass breaking.

DOC: Give me a clean glass, Mac.

The other men at the bar back away out of frame.

BARTENDER *(with concern)*: You're not goin' to start drinkin' whiskey again, are ya?
DOC *(brutally)*: Gimme a glass, Mac!

Chihuahua has turned at the sound of the glass breaking, and now she moves over to the far end of the bar. She is the only other person besides Doc at the bar.

BARTENDER *(producing a glass and a bottle of whiskey from beneath the bar)*: I'm pouring.

Medium shot from behind Doc toward bartender. Doc grabs the bottle and fills the glass.

BARTENDER *(reproachfully)*: Doc! That stuff'll kill ya.

Long shot of Chihuahua at the end of the bar and the musicians on the stand. She begins to sing, walking alongside the bar, swaying with the music. Camera pans with her until Doc comes into frame.

CHIHUAHUA: Oh, the first kiss is always the sweetest
                From under a broad sombrero.

Now that she is next to Doc, she sings the same words again, this time more slowly and seductively, while leaning against him. Then she raises herself

slightly by leaning on the bar, turns her face in front of Doc, and kisses him on the lips.
Medium close-up shows Chihuahua gradually moving her head away, revealing a stony-faced Doc, completely unresponsive to her kiss.

DOC *(slowly, emphatically)*: Why don't you go away. Squall your stupid little songs, and leave me alone.

He swallows another drink, flicks the cap of the whiskey bottle out with his thumb, and fills his glass again.
Chihuahua, looking hurt and resentful, turns slowly and walks back down the bar as the camera pans with her. When she reaches the end of the bar, she turns, grabs a glass, and throws it back in the direction of Doc, off-screen. Sound of glass breaking. The musicians stop playing.
Medium shot of table where the Earps are eating. Wyatt gets up, puts on his hat.

WYATT: Let me see if I can get Doc to bed.

Wyatt walks around the table and exits in foreground, heading toward the bar.

MORGAN *(turning in his chair as Wyatt leaves):* Aw, why don't you finish your supper.

Medium shot looking at Doc from over the bar. Wyatt enters frame on right and settles in next to Doc.

DOC: Have a drink.
WYATT: No thanks, Doc.
DOC *(aggressively)*: I said, have a drink.
WYATT *(amiably)*: No, thanks, I just finished supper. *(Doc fills his own glass again.)* Look, Doc, I ain't tryin' to poke my nose into your personal affairs, but from where I stand, a man would have to go a long ways before he'd find a finer girl than that Miss Carter, or a prettier one, for that matter. There ain't a man west of the Mississippi who wouldn't give his shirt to . . .
DOC *(interrupting)*: Marshal, you've said enough.

WYATT: Just as you say, Doc.

Wyatt stares down at his hands, then across to Doc's glass as Doc fills it again. Doc notices where Wyatt is looking.

DOC: And this isn't any of your business either.

Doc tosses down another drink. He begins to cough and pulls out the white handkerchief to cover the cough.

WYATT *(not looking at Doc)*: Keep that up and you'll be out of business.
DOC *(turning to Wyatt)*: You've just given me a brilliant idea, Marshal. It's time I tempted fate. *(He draws his gun and half turns out from the bar.) (in a louder voice)* Let's see, who's in here I don't particularly like.

Long shot of men sitting at tables, looking over in Doc's direction.
   Return to two shot at the bar, with Doc turned almost completely away from the camera.

WYATT: That's a sucker's game, Doc. (CU *Wyatt*) There's probably fifty fellas around town just waitin' to see you get lickered up so they can fill ya full of holes. (CU *Doc*) Build themselves up a great reputation. (CU *Wyatt*) The man that killed (CU *Doc*) Doc Holliday.

Doc's face tightens.
   Long shot of the bar from the front of the saloon. Doc steps away from the bar and fires, aiming across the saloon and toward the ceiling.
   Long shot of the men at the tables; they scatter as a ceiling lamp comes crashing down.
   Long shot of bar with only Doc and Wyatt in front of bar. Wyatt turns and hits Doc on the jaw, knocking him down and out. The bartender vaults over the bar.

WYATT *(quietly, to bartender)*: Mac, gimme a hand; let's get him to bed.
   (They both bend over Doc.)

Medium shot of piano player seen from the back. He is looking over his shoulder, then turns back to piano and begins playing "Oh, Dem Golden Slippers" at a fast tempo. Scene fades out.

Long establishing shot of Tombstone from the road outside of town. Bells can be heard on the soundtrack. A string of covered wagons comes along the road, heading for town.

Medium shot looking out from Bon Ton Tonsorial Parlor.[22] *In the foreground, Wyatt sits in the barber's chair, his hair wet and slicked down. The barber leans forward in front of Wyatt, holding a mirror so that he can inspect himself. Through the open doors we can see a couple standing with their three young children on the sidewalk; all are dressed in Sunday clothes. Another family comes up to them; there are bows and greetings.*

Medium close-up of Wyatt from behind the barber's mirror. He looks somewhat suspiciously into the mirror. He reaches up and touches the part in his hair, looks again, then reaches up with his other hand to pat the other side of his head.

Medium shot from behind Wyatt of barber holding the mirror, with Wyatt's face reflected in it.

WYATT *(doubtfully)*: You don't think that's kind of . . .
BARBER *(vehemently)*: No sir! No sir!

The barber crosses behind the chair and disappears out of frame for a moment. Long shot as Wyatt gets up and adjusts his coat. The barber reappears, handing Wyatt his hat. Bells continue to sound, and in the street, people and wagons can be seen passing, all moving in one direction.

The barber holds up the mirror to Wyatt for one last inspection, as Wyatt puts on his hat in the doorway.

BARBER: New chair gets in next week—from Kansas City, Kansas.
WYATT *(as he turns to the street)*: Fine, fine.

Barber comes up behind Wyatt with an atomizer, sprays first one side of the back of his neck, then the other.

BARBER: Sweet smellin' stuff, Mr. Earp. Sweet smellin' stuff.

Wyatt rubs the back of his neck, then looks at his hand. He walks out onto the sidewalk.

Long shot down the sidewalk. Wyatt stands alone, while on the street the procession of people continues, on foot, on horseback, in wagons.

Pan shot from edge of sidewalk follows Wyatt as he moves down the sidewalk, holding as he stops before a window to adjust his hat in its reflection. He then walks out of frame.

Reverse long shot down the sidewalk from behind Wyatt. When he reaches the entrance to the Mansion House, Old Dad rushes out carrying a chair, which he places near the porch post. Wyatt sits down, propping one foot on the post and tilting the chair back. It is obviously a favorite spot for him, since it is the same place and pose in which we saw him the preceding day when the stage arrived.

Medium shot of Wyatt from in front of the porch. Morgan and Virgil enter from rear, having come out of the Mansion House. They stand on each side of Wyatt, but farther forward, at the very edge of the porch. All three are dressed in suits, their Sunday clothes.

WYATT: Have a good breakfast?

MORGAN: Yeah. I stowed away a whole skilletful of ham and eggs. Feels good.

VIRGIL: We figured on getting a buckboard and maybe goin' up and see James.

WYATT: Good idea. Figured I might ride out there later this afternoon myself.

Wyatt gets up and joins his brothers standing on the edge of the porch.

Long shot from edge of road outside of town as wagons make the turn onto the road heading straight into Tombstone.

Return to the medium shot of the three Earps.

VIRGIL: If I wasn't in the territory, I'd swear we were back home on a Sunday morning.

WYATT: Yeah, with Ma scrubbin' our necks to go to camp meetin'.

MORGAN: By golly, I'll bet that's what it is—a camp meetin'!

VIRGIL: Could be. You know, I swear I can almost smell the honeysuckle blossoms.

WYATT: That's me. *(His brothers turn to look at him inquiringly.)* Barber.

Long shot of Mansion House from across the street. A buckboard pulls up in front of the Earps. Mr. Simpson and his sister are in front, his sister holding the reins. His wife and three children are in the back.

SIMPSON *(heartily)*: Good mornin'!
WYATT *(as he and Virgil tip their hats)*: Mornin'.
SIMPSON: You gentlemen comin' to church this mornin', I hope. *(The Earps do not respond.)* Well, we're havin' our first social gatherin' . . . to raise enough money to finish the church.
MORGAN *(to Wyatt)*: See, what'd I tell you, it's a camp meetin'.

Medium shot of the buckboard from in front of the Mansion House.

SIMPSON *(very indignant)*: Camp meetin'! No such a dad-blasted thing! *(His wife pulls at his sleeve from the back seat and says admonishingly "Paw!")* Regular church.

Medium shot of the three Earps.

WYATT: Oh, is that what they're buildin'. I was wonderin' what that fresh-cut lumber was for.

Reverse shot of the buckboard.

SIMPSON: Yes, sir! Roof'll be on next week.
MRS. SIMPSON: Yes, I was hopin' that you single men would come. It'll be awful nice for the dancin'.
SIMPSON: Yeah, Sis here is single. *(He gives a belly laugh and elbows his sister, a small elderly woman. She elbows him back vigorously.)* Dad-blasted good dancer, too.

Medium shot of the three Earps.

WYATT: Well, thank ya, ma'am, but my brothers got sort of a job of work to do and I oughta stay around the place.

Reverse shot of buckboard.

SIMPSON: Well, keepin' the peace is no whit less important. *(turns)* Get goin', Sis. *(to Earps)* Good-day. *(He is echoed by his wife.)*

Medium shot of the Earps. They tip their hats as the wagon moves out.

MORGAN: You know, there's probably a lot of nice people around here. We just ain't met 'em.

VIRGIL: Come on, Morg, let's get started. I'd kinda like to get back for that dancin'.

They both exit to the left of the frame.
Long shot down the long porch, with Virgil and Morgan coming toward the camera.[23] *They pass Chihuahua walking in the other direction, with a pitcher of milk in her hand. As Morgan approaches her, he begins to whinny, and she throws the contents of the pitcher in his face. Morgan exits near the camera, spluttering and wiping the milk from his face and his suit. Chihuahua continues down the porch toward the Mansion House, where Earp is sitting in front of the hotel door, tilted back in his chair, keeping his balance with one foot on the porch post.*
Long shot in front of Wyatt, with Chihuahua now standing behind him.

CHIHUAHUA *(indignantly)*: And as for you, when Doc finds out you butted him last night, he'll twist that tin badge around your heart.

As Chihuahua speaks, Wyatt performs a more elaborate balancing act, changing from one foot on the post to the other, spreading out his arms. Chihuahua stares at him, then tosses her head and goes into the hotel. Wyatt stops his performance, half turns his head to look at where Chihuahua had been standing, and smiles.

Long shot looking down the upstairs corridor of the hotel. Chihuahua comes up the stairs, empties out the last of the milk from the pitcher onto the corridor floor, then approaches Doc's door and looks across at the door opposite, the one to the room occupied by Clementine. She hestitates a moment, then opens that door.
Long shot from inside Clementine's room. She is in the foreground with her clothes and her suitcases before her on the bed. She is packing. She turns when

*the door is flung open. The two women look at one another; then Chihuahua
leans against the door frame.*

CHIHUAHUA: I'm Chihuahua. I'm Doc Holliday's girl. Just wanted to make
sure you were packing.

*Chihuahua moves across the hall to Doc's door. Clementine crosses from the
bedside and closes her door.*
   Long shot of the interior of Doc's room.[24] *Chihuahua opens the door, puts
the pitcher down on the dresser, and lets the door slam behind her. The camera
pans with her as she crosses to where Doc lies in bed, one hand on his
forehead. We hear the sound of the pitcher breaking on the floor, presumably
jarred off the dresser by the slamming of the door.*

DOC *(agitatedly)*: Stop slamming doors . . . people dropping pitchers on the
floor . . . no rest.

Chihuahua sits on the bed and embraces him.

CHIHUAHUA: I'm sorry, darling. You're not mad, are you?

DOC *(quieting down)*: Sure not. What right have I got to be mad, at anyone or anything.

Medium shot across the bed of Doc and Chihuahua in profile.

CHIHUAHUA: She's packin', Doc. She's leavin' town.
DOC: Happy, aren't you?
CHIHUAHUA *(sighs, nestles closer to Doc)*: I ain't sad.
DOC *(motioning toward the table at the foot of the bed)*: Get me a drink, huh?

Long shot of the table. Chihuahua looks for a glass, notices the broken glass covering the medical diploma, gets down on her knees, and fishes around under the foot of the bed. She emerges with a glass, sighs, wipes it on her dress, and pours Doc a drink.
   Return to the medium shot across the bed. Chihuahua hands Doc the drink.

DOC: Chihuahua, I'm going into Mexico for a week or ten days. And while I'm gone I want you to . . .
CHIHUAHUA: Take me with you, Doc, will ya?
DOC *(laughs, pleased with the idea)*: Why not? *(He tosses down his drink.)* Why not? Tell François to fix a bridal breakfast—flowers, champagne. You get in your prettiest dress. Tell him the Queen is dead. Long live the Queen.
CHIHUAHUA: Oh . . . Oh, Doc! *(She puts her arms around his neck and gives him a long passionate kiss on the lips.)*

———————

Long shot of the hotel lobby looking across toward the dining room. Clementine comes down the stairs, carrying her bags. She stops at the desk, looks around the empty room, and rings the service bell twice. When there is no response, she leaves her bags by the desk, crosses to a settee near the entrance and sits down facing the desk.
   Medium shot of Clementine discretely wiping away a tear.
   Return to long shot across the lobby. Wyatt walks in through the front door. He is whistling "My Darling Clementine." At first he does not see Clementine and stands there adjusting his hat, as he had done in the barber shop. When he realizes she is sitting there, he takes off his hat and goes over to stand in front of her.

WYATT: Morning, Miss Carter.

CLEMENTINE: Good morning, Mr. Earp.

WYATT: You leavin'?

CLEMENTINE: Yes, I'm leaving for the East on the stage.

WYATT: The east-bound stage don't leave till noon on Sunday. It's a mighty short visit.

CLEMENTINE: Some people think I've overstayed my visit already.

Medium shot of Wyatt.

WYATT: I dunno, ma'am, but if you ask me I think you're givin' up too easy.

CLEMENTINE (MS) *(without looking at Wyatt)*: Marshal, if you ask me, I don't think you know too much about a woman's pride.

Return to long shot of the lobby, as church bells begin to sound. A group of women who work at the hotel enter from the door at the back of the dining room; they are dressed for church, and they cross the dining room and go out the front door.

WYATT: No ma'am, maybe I don't.

The hotel clerk follows after the women.

CLERK *(calling after them)*: Girls, don't forget to be back in time for Sunday dinner, now.

Clementine has gotten up and now she and Wyatt stand by the front door.

CLERK *(noticing the luggage)*: Oh, I'm sorry about your bags, Miss Carter. I didn't have a chance to get 'em down. The girls put together a packet of lunch and . . .

MAYOR *(coming down the stairs and overlapping with the clerk's words)*: Bless my soul, he did it. Good morning, Miss. Good morning, Marshal. John Simpson said he'd have a church and he has.

Medium shot of the Mayor joining Clementine and Wyatt just inside the hotel door.

MAYOR *(with a touch of wonder)*: Church bells in Tombstone.

CLEMENTINE: I believe that's the first church bell I've heard in months.

MAYOR *(agreeably)*: Yeah. *(He looks at both Clementine and Wyatt, but they are silent, looking out into the street.)*

MAYOR *(uncertain)*: Well . . . *(He puts on his hat and walks out.)*

Long shot of the porch. The Mayor comes out of the hotel and walks toward the camera. Behind him, Wyatt and Clementine also come out of the hotel.

Medium shot of Wyatt and Clementine at the edge of the porch in front of the hotel. They are standing in bright sunlight.[25]

CLEMENTINE *(looking around)*: I love your town in the morning, Marshal. The air is so clean and clear. *(She breathes deeply.)* The scent of the desert flowers.

WYATT *(slightly uncomfortable)*: That's me. *(He nods in the direction of the Bon Ton.)* Barber.

CLEMENTINE *(turning to Wyatt)*: Marshal, may I go with you? *(Distant voices singing "Shall We Gather at The River" join the continuing sound of the church bells; Wyatt looks blank.)* You are going to the services, aren't you?

WYATT *(recovering himself)*: Yes, ma'am. I'd admire to take you.

CLEMENTINE: Thank you.

Wyatt offers his arm, she takes it, and they turn and walk out of the frame.

Long shot down the porch from the corner. Wyatt and Clementine slowly advance toward the camera as the hymn grows slightly louder on the sound track. As they reach the corner, near the camera, they turn to the right.

Long shot looking at the couple as they turn into the long porch of the cross street, passing the barber standing in front of his shop at the corner. He salutes them with a wave. The camera is positioned just off the edge of the porch, so it looks toward the couple from a slight angle. As they walk, the camera tracks with them, keeping some distance ahead of them.

Long shot of the shell of the church, with the skeleton of a church tower outlined against the sky. American flags fly in the breeze, and people and horses and wagons are clustered below.

Long shot of Wyatt and Clementine; they have now passed beyond the end of the porch and the connected town buildings and are walking in the open space beyond. The camera holds as they approach and pass out of the frame to the right.

Long shot of the church structure outlined in the distance. In the foreground, Wyatt and Clementine are seen from the back as they walk slowly away from the camera and toward the church tower.

Medium shot of John Simpson, standing at a lectern, with a violin bow in his hand.

SIMPSON: Now, folks, I hereby declare the First Church of Tombstone, which ain't got no name yet nor no preacher either, officially dedicated. Now I don't pretend to be no preacher, but I've read the good book from cover to cover and back again, and I've nary found one word agin dancin'. So we'll commence by havin' a dad-blasted good dance!

He picks up the violin to cheers from the crowd, steps out from the lectern, stomps a tempo with his foot, and begins to play.

Low-angle long shot from in front of the platform where Simpson and the other musicians are playing.

Long shot from above the church area. On the open floor of the church—the sides and roof have yet to be constructed—people are dancing. In the fore-

ground, two American flags are whipping in the breeze. Behind the church stretches the open Arizona country, with the mesas in the distance.

Another long shot follows, from a slightly different angle, which brings the camera closer to the dancers.

Return to the shot of the musicians on the platform.

Close-up of Old Dad, playing the violin.

Medium shot of the musicians, seen from the back of the platform. Mac, the bartender, is in the foreground, playing an upright piano. The crowd supports the music with rhythmic clapping throughout the entire sequence.

Long shot of the dancers. There are facing lines of men and women; individual dancers meet a partner between the lines, each in turn, according to the music, and then go back to their places. The camera looks down the line of dancers, slightly angled toward the women's line.

Long shot looking directly down the space between the two lines. The dancers move across the frame, circling and turning. At the far end of the space, the bottom of the steeple frame can be seen.

Medium shot of Wyatt and Clementine watching the dancers.

Return to previous shot of the dancers.
Low angle shot of the floor of the platform, with the musicians' booted feet tapping out the rhythm.
Return to the previous shot of the dancers.
Medium shot of Wyatt and Clementine. She is now clapping along with the music. She looks up at Wyatt with amusement and some expectation; he stares out at the dancers. Then he notices her clapping her hands.
Another shot of the dancers as the men and women move into the center area in pairs.
Long shot of the dance floor from above, this time with the town of Tombstone and the country beyond it in the background.
Return to the medium shot of Wyatt and Clementine. He still stares ahead, while she watches the dancers and occasionally glances at him, suppressing a smile. He takes off his hat, holds it in his hand for a moment, then tosses it away. He turns to her.

WYATT *(with a visible effort)*: Oblige me, ma'am.
CLEMENTINE *(smiling)*: Thank you. *(She removes her shawl and gives it to Wyatt, who folds it on his arm. She takes his arm and they walk out of the frame.)*

Long shot from behind Wyatt and Clementine as they walk toward the floor where the dancers are in motion. When they reach the raised floor, Wyatt offers Clementine his arm as she steps up.

SIMPSON *(off-screen)*: Hold it folks! Dad-blast it, hold it!

Medium shot of Simpson holding his violin.

SIMPSON: Sashay back, and make room for our new Marshal *(with a courtly bow)* and his lady fair.

Medium shot of Wyatt and Clementine. Wyatt bows awkwardly, then puts his arm around Clementine, and prepares to dance. The music strikes up again.
Long shot of the dance floor. The other dancers have now formed a circle and watch as Wyatt and Clementine dance by themselves. The crowd is clapping and cheering. The camera pans to follow the pair as they circle on the floor. A cut brings the camera slightly closer.

Long shot of a carriage approaching and pulling up in front of the camera. Virgil and Morgan stare out in amazement.

Another shot of the dance floor, this time much closer to the two dancers, the camera tilted up from a slightly lower angle. Wyatt and Clementine are obviously enjoying themselves.

Medium shot of Morgan and Virgil, sitting on the buggy.

MORGAN: Well, by golly!

Long shot of Wyatt and Clementine dancing, as the scene fades.[26]

Long shot of the hotel dining room, crowded with Sunday diners. Wyatt is standing at the nearest table, facing the camera, and he is carving some fowl. Seated at the table are Clementine and Mr. and Mrs. Simpson.

SIMPSON: Marshal, I hope you're as good a dad-blasted carver as you are a dad-blasted good dancer. *(The others laugh. The room is filled with noise and good humor.)*

Long shot of the bottom of the hotel staircase. Doc comes down, dressed in his Western outfit, the one he wore in his first appearance in the Oriental Saloon. He goes to the desk to leave his key and, looking off-screen, he sees Clementine in the dining room.
      Return to previous shot of the dining room. Doc comes to stand at the table.

DOC: Pardon me for intruding on your dinner party, Marshal.
WYATT: That's all right, Doc. Sit down and join us.
DOC: Look, Clem, I told you last night to leave Tombstone and go back East. I also told you if you didn't leave, I would.[27]

Doc stalks away from the table and out of the frame.

WYATT: Hey, Doc! *(He moves after Holliday.)*

Medium shot of the front door of the hotel. Doc waits there for Wyatt, who walks slowly up to him.

WYATT: Just a minute, Doc. That's the second time in three days you've been trying to run somebody out of town. That's my business. That's what I'm gettin' paid for. Miss Carter or any other decent citizen can stay here just as long as they want to.
DOC: We're through talking, Marshal. My advice to you is start carrying your gun.
WYATT: That's good advice.

Doc brushes past Wyatt and exits frame right. Wyatt pauses for a moment, then slowly walks back into the hotel.[28]

Slow dissolve to medium close-up of Chihuahua standing in a doorway. She reacts to something off-screen, then moves out of the frame.
      Long shot of the porch and street. Chihuahua stops at the edge of the porch as the stagecoach comes into view, moving very fast, and speeds by her. As it passes her, one of the men on the driver's seat throws something down into the street.
      Long shot from behind Chihuahua looking out into the street in the opposite direction, following the rear of the departing stage.

Medium shot of the two men on the driver's seat. The man riding shotgun is Doc. He looks back in Chihuahua's direction, then turns forward again. He strains ahead in his seat, then throws a stone at the horses to urge them to go faster.

Long shot from the porch behind Chihuahua. She goes into the street and picks up what Doc has thrown to her.

Close up of a moneybag labeled "Cattlemen's Savings Bank, Tucson, Arizona."

Long shot from the porch of Chihuahua in the street, looking at the bag in her hand. The camera pans to follow her as she moves back to the porch, calls out "Mamacita," and throws the bag through the doorway. The camera holds as Chihuahua begins to run down the long porch toward the center of town, moving away from the camera.

Long shot from the street; camera pans as Chihuahua continues running past the cross street and the barber shop and then turns into the Mansion House entrance.

Long shot of the interior of Clementine's room. She is unpacking her bag, with her door open. Chihuahua appears in the doorway.

CHIHUAHUA: Doc's gone.

Medium shot of Chihuahua in the doorway.

CHIHUAHUA: He's left town. He was goin' to Mexico. He was takin' me with him. He was gonna marry me.

A return to the previous long shot, with Clementine in the foreground.

CHIHUAHUA *(angrily)*: Well, you're leaving, too.[29]

She goes over the the clothes rack and takes all the dresses there and tosses them on the bed. Then she turns and opens the drawer of the dresser behind the door to the room. As she leans over the dresser, Wyatt appears in the doorway, raising his hat to Clementine. Then he sees Chihuahua with her hands filled with Clementine's belongings.

WYATT *(entering)*: What's the matter, Miss Carter?

CLEMENTINE: Well, I think it's just a common case of hysteria, Marshal.
CHIHUAHUA *(facing her)*: Oh, it is, is it?
WYATT: What are you doin' here?
CHIHUAHUA: None of your business!
WYATT: Why don't you behave yourself. Get out, go on back where you belong.
CHIHUAHUA: I'm not gettin' out till she leaves town.

Chihuahua lunges at Clementine. Wyatt grabs her from behind by the arms.
Medium shot of Chihuahua with Wyatt behind her. He swings her around and pushes into the doorway.

WYATT: You want me to take you on my knee and spank you?
CHIHUAHUA *(breaking free)*: You take your hands off me. Leave me alone. What do you know about it anyway? What do you know about Doc and me? We was goin' to Mexico and get married. Yes, he was gonna marry me! Until this Miss Mealface comes pussyfootin' along an' . . .

As she speaks Wyatt notices the cross she is wearing around her neck. When he holds the object on the chain to look at it, Chihuahua slaps his arm, and the chain breaks, leaving the cross in Wyatt's hand.

WYATT: Where'd you get that?
CHIHUAHUA *(rubbing her neck and very angry)*: Doc gave it to me. Where do you think I got it?
WYATT: You ain't lyin'?
CHIHUAHUA: Why should I lie about it? He gives me everything I've got. I got a whole roomful of stuff down there. *(She is very agitated; Wyatt pushes her out the door.)*

Long shot down the corridor. Morgan is walking toward the camera from the staircase, as Wyatt and Chihuahua enter the corridor.

WYATT *(back to Clementine)*: Keep your door locked. *(to Morgan)* Keep this wildcat locked in her room for awhile, will ya, and tell Virg to stick around.
MORGAN: What's up?

Wyatt shows him the cross, then starts toward the stairs.

WYATT: Doc Holliday.

Dissolve to a long shot of the saloon, looking along the bar toward the front door. Wyatt enters and walks over to the bar. The room is empty. The bartender comes over to him.

WYATT: Where's Holliday?
BARTENDER: Came in about half an hour ago, got his saddlebags and a sack of gold out of the safe and left in a hurry.

The Clantons walk into the shot from the side, moving up to the bar, with Old Man Clanton closest to Wyatt.
   Medium shot of Wyatt and the bartender both looking down toward the Clantons.
   Reverse shot of the five Clantons staring at Wyatt.
   Long shot of the saloon door. The Mayor enters and the camera pans with him as he walks over to Wyatt.

MAYOR: Were you looking for Doc?
WYATT: I am.
MAYOR: Well, he left on the bullion stage, riding shotgun.
WYATT: Left town?
MAYOR: For Tucson.
WYATT: Get my bay mare and have her up the jail, will ya, Jess?

The camera pans to follow Wyatt as he, and then the Mayor, go out the door.
   Long shot of the Clantons lined up at the bar. Old Man Clanton strikes the bar with his whip.

CLANTON *(roughly, to bartender)*: You! Whiskey! For my boys.

They turn to face toward the bar and away from the camera as the scene dissolves.

Dissolve to a long establishing shot of rugged Arizona country. A stagecoach is coming rapidly toward the camera; the camera pans to follow it as it goes by.
   Long shot looking down the road as the stagecoach moves rapidly away from the camera.

Long shot of the Tombstone jail and yard. Wyatt and the Mayor are walking from the jail to where a horse is waiting.

MAYOR: I think the Wachuca Pass is your best bet, Wyatt. Good luck.
WYATT *(mounting his horse)*: Thank you, Jess. *(Wyatt rides off.)*

Long shot from the jail yard with the Mayor watching as Wyatt rides directly out into open country.
   Low-angle long shot of Wyatt riding away from the camera.
   Long shot of flat desert country. Wyatt rides into the frame in the foreground and continues to ride away from the camera.
   Long shot of the stagecoach moving along the road.
   Medium shot of the stage driver and Doc, who is still urging the horses on. Dissolve to
   Long shot from behind the entrance gate to the Wells Fargo Corral. Men stand by the gate and look out along the road. Wyatt comes down the road, riding very hard, and turns in through the open gate. The men close the gate after he passes through.
   Long shot of Wyatt dismounting, seen from behind. The corral men gather around the horse.

WYATT *(to one of the men)*: Indigo, how long ago did the stage come through
   here?
INDIGO: Why, about fifteen or twenty minutes ago.
WYATT *(as he removes his saddle)*: Doc Holliday on it?
INDIGO: Yes, he was, and he was sure goin' to town.
WYATT *(as the men lead his horse away)*: I need a couple of fresh horses. Cut
   me out two stout ones, will ya, Joe? One that'll lead well.
INDIGO: All right, Marshal.

Medium shot of Wyatt with a ladle at the water bucket.
   Long shot of a cowboy on horseback at the corral lassoing a horse to cut it out of the herd.

WYATT *(off-screen)*: That bay looks good.

Dissolve to a long shot of a flat stretch of road, with the stagecoach approaching. It passes the camera in a cloud of dust.

Dissolve to a long shot of a rocky hillside, with Wyatt descending on horseback, leading another horse, and riding directly toward the camera.

Another long shot of the coach on flat terrain, speeding along. Doc can be heard shouting at the horses.

Medium shot of Doc and the driver, with Doc shouting at the horses.

Medium shot of the lead horses.

Return to the shot of Doc and the driver. Doc seems out of control; he grabs at the reins to push the horses on.

Another medium shot of the lead horses.

Close-up of a rear wheel of the stage, almost invisible in the dust.

Long shot of Wyatt riding on flat land; the camera tracks with him.

Low angle shot of the approaching stage.

Medium shot of Doc and the driver.

Another shot of the lead horses.

Low-angle long shot of the coach and horses; it is close enough to make out Doc's figure, but most of the coach is concealed by dust.

Close-up of the rear wheel, now barely visible at all because of the dust.

Long shot of Wyatt riding up an incline at the end of a long stretch of flatland.

Long shot of the rear of the coach as it climbs up an incline. The rear of the coach disappears in the dust.

Long shot of Wyatt descending; the landscape is extremely rugged and bare. The sounds of his horses now mingle with the sounds of the coach.

Long shot of the coach, now also descending on the road.

Long shot of Wyatt approaching the camera. He reins in his horses.

Long shot of the coach in side view.

Long shot from in front of Wyatt; he is stationary on his horse in the road.

WYATT *(raising his hand)*: Pull up!

Long shot of the coach seen from the side; it comes to a halt.

Long shot from in front of the lead horses as they pull up.

Long shot from the side across the top of the horses toward Doc and the driver. The driver is pulling on the reins and shouting "Whoa!"

Long shot of Wyatt, who now dismounts and places the reins of his horse under a rock.

Low-angle long shot looking up at the driver's seat. Doc takes off his coat, jumps down from the stage on the side away from the camera.

Long shot of Wyatt walking toward the camera.
Long shot from behind Wyatt of Doc, walking by the coach horses toward Wyatt.

DOC: I told you I'm through talking, Marshal.
WYATT: You're coming back to Tombstone with me, Doc.

Medium close-up of Doc.

DOC: Sorry, I'm not going back.

Medium close-up of Wyatt.

WYATT: Well, in that case, I'll be taking you back.

Long shot from behind Wyatt. Doc stands in front of the coach horses.

DOC: Go for your gun, Marshal.
WYATT: You call it, Doc.

They begin to walk toward each other. Doc draws first, but Wyatt fires the only shot. Doc grabs his gun hand and pulls it up to his face in pain.[30]

Medium shot of the wall of Chihuahua's room. Sounds are heard of someone knocking urgently on a door. Chihuahua moves into the frame and faces the camera. She is adjusting her blouse.

CHIHUAHUA: Who is it?
WYATT *(off-screen)*: The Marshal.
CHIHUAHUA *(angrily)*: Why don't you go chase yourself up an alley! Who do you think you are, busting into people's rooms . . .
DOC *(off-screen, interrupting)*: Chihuahua, open this door!
CHIHUAHUA *(startled)*: Doc? *(Billy Clanton passes behind her.)* Is that you, Doc?

Billy can be seen behind Chihuahua, putting on his hat, and then drawing his gun.

DOC *(off-screen)*: I said open this door!
CHIHUAHUA: Yeah, Doc. Yeah. Just a minute.

*She turns and pushes Billy's gun, which he is pointing toward the door, aside.
She opens a long window that gives out on the roof of the building and pushes
Billy through it.*

DOC *(off-screen)*: Chihuahua! Chihuahua! Open this door before I kick it
down!
CHIHUAHUA *(turning back into the room, obviously rattled)*: Yeah, Doc.
Lemme get something on.

Medium shot of Wyatt and Doc, seen from behind, outside Chihuahua's door.

DOC: Well, hurry up! *(He begins to kick the door and beat on it with his fists.)*

*Medium shot of Chihuahua at the door, listening to Doc pounding and shout-
ing. She pauses at the door for a moment, then unlocks it and steps back. The
camera pans with her.*

CHIHUAHUA: Come in, Doc.

*Medium shot from outside the door of Doc and Wyatt entering.
   Medium shot of Chihuahua. Doc enters the frame on the left, and she turns
to face him.*

DOC *(abruptly)*: Chihuahua, why did you tell the Marshal I gave you this
jewelry?

Wyatt enters the frame behind and between them.

CHIHUAHUA *(nervously)*: Well, you did, Doc. You gave it to me.
DOC *(very angry)*: I never saw this piece of junk before in my life. Who gave
it to you?
CHIHUAHUA: Well, you can't remember everything you give me, Doc. Sure
you did, don't you remember?
DOC: When?

CHIHUAHUA *(looking back and forth at the two men)*: Er . . . two or three
   days ago, I don't know. What difference does it make?
WYATT: That being the case, Doc, I charge you with the murder of my brother,
   James Earp.
CHIHUAHUA *(after a pause)*: Doc, he's foolin'.
WYATT: I ain't foolin'. *(staring hard at her)* It was stolen from him the night
   he was shot in the back.

*Chihuahua looks stunned. She puts her hand to her throat where she had worn
the cross, then walks between the two men to the far side of the room. The
camera pans with her. The two men follow her.*

DOC: Now do you still insist I gave it to you.
CHIHUAHUA *(still with her back to them)*: No, no, of course not.
WYATT *(behind her)*: Then who did?
CHIHUAHUA *(turning)*: I ain't gonna be a squealer, Doc.
WYATT *(reaching over and taking Doc's gun from his holster)*: Let's go, Doc.

*Chihuahua turns again, looks at Doc, then drops down on her bed. She sits
between the two standing men, sobs once, and uses her skirt to wipe her eyes.*

CHIHUAHUA (CU, *looking up at Doc*): Well, you told me to go away and
   squall my silly little songs somewhere else, so I came up here and had a
   good cry. *(She looks down)* There was a knock at the door and I thought it
   was you. I opened the door and *(long pause)* it was Billy Clanton.[31]

*Long shot looking down on the bed from behind Doc. Gunshots are heard. Chi-
huahua collapses on the bed. Doc leans over her.*
   *Long shot of the flat roof outside Chihuahua's window. Billy stands next to
the window, firing. Then he dashes along the roof toward the camera.*
   *Long shot of the edge of the roof seen from across the street at street level.
Billy reaches the edge of the roof and makes the one-story jump into the street.
The camera pans with him as he crosses the street to where his horse is hitched
and mounts it.*[32]
   *Long shot from the roof looking down into the street. Billy has turned out
into the main street and is starting to ride out of town. Wyatt enters the frame
and fires. Billy slumps on his horse, but keeps riding.*

Medium shot of Wyatt firing again.
Long shot of Virgil on horseback pulling up in the street as he hears Wyatt
firing again off-screen.
Return to medium shot of Wyatt firing again. He hears the sound of hoof-
beats and looks down below.

WYATT: Billy Clanton! Go get him, Virg!

Medium shot of Virgil looking up at Wyatt, then spurring his horse and riding
away.
Long shot from the roof looking from behind Wyatt as he watches Virgil in
the distance riding hard in pursuit.
Low-angle long shot from the roadway, as Billy rides by, firing behind him.
The same shot from the same location, but now with Virgil riding by, still in
pursuit.
Medium shot of the door of Chihuahua's room from inside the room. Wyatt
opens the door; a crowd has gathered outside. They begin to push in, led by
Mac, the bartender. The Mayor and Morgan follow.

VOICE: What happened?
WYATT: There's been a shooting. Stay outside, fellas. *(He closes the door.)*
DOC *(coming into the frame as he rises from the bedside)*: Wyatt, she's badly
    hurt. Mayor, you'd better send to Wachuca for an army doctor. We need to
    operate immediately.
MAYOR: That'll take five or six hours, Doc.
WYATT: You're a doctor, ain't ya?
DOC *(ironically)*: Doctor! *(He turns back to the bedside.)*

Medium shot across the bed. Doc kneels at the side of the bed, while a Mexi-
can woman brings over some towels. Morgan and Wyatt stand behind Doc,
and a man next to him holds a kerosene lamp.

WYATT: Morg, go over to the Mansion House and get Miss Carter. She's a nurse.
    Tell her to stop by Doc's room and get that doctor's bag. *(Morgan leaves.)*
    Mac, you and Buck go down and clean up the saloon. Put a couple of poker
    tables together and put some lights around 'em. *(Doc rises and turns to face*
    Wyatt.)

WYATT: Doc, you're gonna operate.[33]

---

*Dissolve to the kitchen of the Oriental Saloon. Long shot of Doc standing be-
hind the kitchen table and washing his hands in a basin. Clementine, dressed
in a nurse's uniform, stands on one side of Doc; Wyatt, pouring alcohol from a
bottle over Doc's hands, stands on the other.*
   *Long shot of the makeshift operating table in the saloon. Lamps are hung
over the table, but the rest of the room is in darkness. A crowd surrounds the
table. Morgan turns from the crowd and the circle of light and walks toward
the camera.*

MORGAN: All ready, Doc!

*Long shot across the darkened back part of the saloon looking toward the kit-
chen door and the lighted kitchen. Wyatt pushes the door open and Clementine
walks out, carrying towels, followed by Doc with his sleeves rolled up and his
hands held in front of him. The camera pans with Doc as he moves into the center
of the saloon.*

DOC: Mac, the light. *(Mac brings a kerosene lamp around the table to Doc.)*
KATE NELSON *(softly, her face hidden from the camera by Mac in the foreground)*: Doc's here, honey. *(to Doc)* She's been right brave.

*Close-up of Chihuahua. Her head is on a pillow and her eyes are closed. She
opens her eyes.*
   Close-up of Doc, looking down. He smiles reassuringly.

CHIHUAHUA (CU) *(softly)*: Sorry, Doc. Still mad?
DOC (MS): No, honey. Look, I haven't got anything to put you to sleep, so this
   is going to hurt like blazes.

*Medium shot of Clementine, within the circle of light. Standing in the shadow
behind her, half turned toward her, is Wyatt.*

DOC *(off-screen)*: Yell, scream, holler, anything you like.

Medium shot of Doc.

DOC *(still softly)*; Tell me when you're ready.

Close-up of Chihuahua. She hesitates, then nods. Kate Nelson's hand appears, holding a piece of folded cloth.

KATE NELSON (MS): Bite on it, bite hard.

Close-up of Chihuahua. She opens her mouth, and the hand inserts the piece of cloth. She bites down. Kate's hand then rests on Chihuahua's forehead.
    Medium shot of Doc. He leans down and forward. As he does, Mac's arm appears in the frame, raising the lamp above Doc's head.
    Long shot from the far end of the saloon. Figures are bent around the lighted area where Doc is operating. Sounds of music and shouts from outside can be heard.

CHIHUAHUA *(in pain)*: Oh, Ma.
KATE: There, there, honey. Doc's gonna help you.

Long shot of Virgil riding hard across the plain toward the camera. Low-angle long shot of Virgil's horse from behind as he rides away from the camera.
    Another long shot of Billy from behind. This time he wheels his horse, fires, then rides away.
    Long shot of Billy coming over a rise.
    Long shot from the door of the Clanton ranch looking out through a small patio to the yard beyond. Hoofbeats are heard, and then Billy rides into the yard.
    Long shot of the Clantons at supper. They look up, hearing the horse. Old Man Clanton and Ike stand up and continue listening.
    Long shot looking out from the Clanton doorway. Billy dismounts, staggering. He manages to walk a few steps, then collapses on the patio.
    Return to previous shot of the Clantons. Old Man Clanton hears the sound of Billy falling, and he moves out of the frame toward the door.
    Close-up of the lower part of the inside of the door. As Old Man Clanton opens it, we see past him to Billy lying on the ground.
    Medium shot of Clanton standing in the doorway. He is looking down at Billy. As we hear the sound of hoofbeats, Clanton raises his head and narrows his eyes.

Long shot of the open plain. The camera pans as Virgil gallops by.
Long shot of Virgil coming over a rise.
Long shot from the Clantons' door, as earlier. Virgil rides into the yard and dismounts. Billy's body is no longer there.
Medium shot of the inside of the Clantons' door. Virgil can be heard knocking. Phin opens the door. Virgil stands there with his gun out; he puts it back in the holster.

VIRGIL: I'm looking for your brother, Billy Clanton.
PHIN: He's right in there, Mr. Earp. *(He motions with his thumb. Virgil goes past him out of the frame.)*

Long shot across a bedroom. Billy Clanton lies stretched out, face up, on the bed. Old Man Clanton is seated on the far side of the bed; Ike and Sam stand on the near side. Virgil enters the room, stops, takes off his hat and stands at the foot of the bed.

CLANTON: My boy, Billy. Shot down on the streets of Tombstone.

Medium shot of Clanton in his chair. He turns to look at Virgil.

CLANTON: Murdered.
VIRGIL (MS): It's too bad it had to end this way, Mr. Clanton.

Return to the long shot across the bed. Virgil turns and leaves the room. Clanton picks up a shotgun.
Medium shot of Virgil in the doorway leaving the bedroom. The sound of a shot. Virgil throws up his hands and falls. As he drops out of the frame, we see Clanton, still sitting in his chair, with the shotgun smoking in his hands. Phin comes in from the foreground, steps over the body of Virgil, and pauses for a moment to look back at it.
Long shot across the bed.

CLANTON: Get mounted!

The Clanton brothers leave the room. Old Man Clanton gets up, puts on his hat, and blows out the lamp. He walks out the door; Billy's body is still visible on the bed, lit by moonlight from the bedroom window.

Close-up of Chihuahua's face on the pillow. Sounds of revelry can be heard faintly from outside.
   Low-angle medium shot of Doc wiping his face with a towel. His face is in shadow, but he is starting to smile.

CHIHUAHUA (CU) *(She smiles, but with an effort.)*: Hi, Doc.

Return to the shot of Doc.

DOC: You're all right. You've been a brave girl.

Return to close-up of Chihuahua.
   Return to medium shot of Doc.
   Long shot of the operating table. Clementine backs away from the table.

CLEMENTINE: All right, lift her up gently now.

A group of men lift Chihuahua and slowly move away from the camera, toward the entrance of the saloon. Clementine accompanies them.
   Medium shot of Kate and Doc facing one another, with Wyatt standing in the background.

KATE: Doc, I mean Doctor. I'm going to take her to my house and take good
   care of her. *(She turns toward Wyatt.)* Can't I do that, Marshal?[34]
WYATT *(smiling)*: Sure.

She smiles up at Holliday, then walks past Wyatt and out of the frame. Doc turns and joins Wyatt at the bar.
   Long shot from behind the bar. Wyatt, with an air of satisfaction, begins slapping his hand on the bar for service. The room appears to be empty except for Doc, Wyatt, and Mac, the bartender. In the background we see the group carrying Chihuahua moving through the front door. Doc leans forward on the bar and breathes out in relief. Wyatt takes a bottle from the bartender and

pours a drink for Holliday and himself. The bartender takes the bottle and pours one for himself.

WYATT *(meaningfully)*: Doctor Holliday.

The bartender begins to chuckle. They all raise their glasses with obvious pleasure. They drink. The bartender chuckles again. Wyatt slides the doctor's bag along the bar to Doc, who picks it up and carries it with him as he walks through the saloon toward the door. Both Wyatt and the bartender turn to watch him as he leaves.

   Medium shot of Clementine holding open the saloon door. As Doc comes to the door, he stops. She looks up at him.

CLEMENTINE: I'm awfully proud of you, John.
DOC: Thanks, Clem. She was a brave girl. *(He turns and walks out.)*

Long shot from behind Wyatt and Mac. They are both watching Clementine as she stands at the saloon door. She bows her head, stays for a moment, then leaves. Wyatt looks down at his drink, then up at the bartender.

WYATT: Mac, you ever been in love?
MAC: No, I been a bartender all me life.

Wyatt downs his drink, then starts to walk toward the front door as the bartender removes the glasses from the top of the bar and disappears from the frame. The camera holds on Wyatt until he pushes through the swinging doors.

   Long shot of Wyatt coming through the doors. Just as he does, a shot rings out, striking one of the lamps inside the saloon. He pulls his gun and fires twice, crouching and retreating back into the saloon.

   Low-angle long shot of three riders coming down the street, leaning close over their saddles, one of them firing toward the camera.

   Low-angle long shot of a single rider approaching, pulling up his horse, and letting a body roll off his saddle pommel to the ground.

   Medium shot of Old Man Clanton, with his horse reined in.

CLANTON *(shouting)*: We'll be waiting for you, Marshal, at the O.K. Corral. *(He turns his horse and rides out of the frame.)*[35]

Long shot of the saloon entrance. Wyatt in shadow comes slowly out onto the porch. The camera pans with him as he begins to run into the road, stopping over the body of Virgil, who is lying face down. As Wyatt bends down, Morgan comes into frame from the other side.

Low-angle medium shot of Wyatt turning the body over and holding Virgil, looking down into his face.

Long shot of all three figures in shadow—Morgan standing, Wyatt kneeling, Virgil in his arms.

Slow dissolve to a long shot of the interior of the jail. Morgan is stripped to the waist and stands in the background, washing his face in the washbasin. Wyatt is seated at a desk in the foreground, facing in the opposite direction, with his feet propped up on the desk. There is a knock on the door. A voice calls "Marshal." Morgan opens the door and the Mayor enters, followed by John Simpson. They gather at the desk where Wyatt is sitting. Morgan goes back to the basin.

MAYOR: Well, the Clantons are at the O.K. Corral, all right. They're barricaded down there, all four of them.

Medium shot, from behind and to the side of Wyatt, looking toward the Mayor and Simpson.

SIMPSON: Marshal, we want you to count us in on this. We ain't fighting men, but we'd sure like to help you out.
WYATT: Thanks, Deacon, but this is strictly a family affair.

Medium shot of Old Man Clanton, leaning over the top of the corral fence, staring out toward Tombstone. He is joined by Ike.

IKE *(his speech a bit slurred)*: What's the matter. They too yeller to come out and fight.
CLANTON: They'll come. *(Ike snorts and turns back into the corral. Clanton looks after him.)* Easy on that keg, son.

Medium shot of the inside of the jailhouse door. Morgan, now with his shirt on, opens the door. Doc enters. He has his holster on.
    Long shot of Wyatt and the Mayor at the desk; Doc joins them.

WYATT: How's Chihuahua?

Medium low angle shot of Doc, who looks at Wyatt, then turns his face away.

DOC: She's dead. *(with scorn)* Doctor John Holliday! *(He takes a shotgun down from the wall, uncocks it, then looks back at Wyatt.)* When do we start?

Long shot of Doc, Wyatt, and the Mayor.

WYATT *(after a pause)*: Sunup.

Dissolve to a medium shot of Old Man Clanton, still at the rail of the corral. His head has dropped down; he is dozing. Now he raises his head. The sky is much lighter than in the previous shot of Clanton. He turns to look back into the corral.

CLANTON: Sunup, Ike! Phin! Sam!

Then he turns back to stare out at the road.

Long shot of the jail office. The men are stirring. Medium shot of the Mayor at the window, looking out.

MAYOR: Sun's coming up, Marshal.

Medium shot of Wyatt at the washbasin. He takes his badge from his vest, which is hanging on the wall; he puts the badge in his trouser pocket and puts on his hat.
    Long shot of the room; Wyatt takes a piece of paper from the Mayor (the warrant for the Clantons) and puts it in his shirt pocket. He reaches down on the desk and picks up a shotgun.
    Medium shot of Wyatt removing shells from the shotgun and handing the empty gun to the Mayor. He then reaches behind the Mayor and takes a second shotgun from the wall, empties that, and gives it to Simpson. He moves over to Morgan, who gives him two handguns. Wyatt hefts them, gives one back to Morgan and keeps the other. Then he turns back to the Mayor and Simpson.[36]

WYATT: Got everything straight?

Long shot of the room.

MAYOR AND SIMPSON: Yeah.

Earp opens the door, the Mayor blows out the lamp, and the five men walk outside.
   Long shot of the entrance to the jail. The five men stand near the door, Wyatt the furthest forward. He turns back to the others.

WYATT: Let's go.

Doc and Morgan walk out of the frame on the left. The Mayor passes Wyatt and goes out of the frame near the camera. Wyatt and then Simpson follow.
   Long shot from the jail yard looking through the gate out into the street. The Mayor is already in the middle of the street, Wyatt is just passing through the gate, and Simpson is just behind Wyatt.
   Long shot of the main road of Tombstone. Wyatt, the Mayor, and Simpson advance down the street, but they are so far from the camera that they look like small black dots on the road.
   Long shot of Sam Clanton braced against the top of a section of the corral rail. He has a shotgun cradled in his arms.

SAM: Here they come!

Long shot of Old Man Clanton seen through the corral rails. He is sitting in a chair, with a shotgun across his lap. He now stands up and begins to walk slowly along behind the corral rail.
   Long shot of Ike and his brother behind another rail. They move closer to the rail and cock their guns.
   Another long shot of the main road, with Wyatt's group in the far distance.
   Medium shot of Old Man Clanton, standing at the rail.

CLANTON: Doc Holliday's with 'em.

Medium shot of Ike and Phin, still leaning on the railing, their guns in front of them.
   High-angle long shot from behind the entrance to the corral. Old Man Clanton is directly behind the gate, Ike and Phin further to the right. The camera looks toward the town and the three small figures walking slowly toward the corral.

Long shot looking across the main street of Tombstone, toward the side with the buildings. In the foreground, on the near side of the street, is a wooden fence. Wyatt walks down the middle of the street, parallel to the camera, with Simpson on his far side and the Mayor on his near side, both slightly behind him. As they come abreast of the camera, the Mayor suddenly runs toward the camera and stops behind the barrier created by the fence. Simpson steps out of the street on the other side and onto the porch.

Long shot down the porch as Simpson steps onto it. He takes a few steps toward the camera, then puts his gun down and stands against the wall.

Medium shot of Wyatt seen from the side, still walking slowly in the middle of the street, and now passing the Mansion House.

Long shot down a narrow alley. Morgan and Doc are moving up the alley with six-guns in their hands. They stop at the end of the alley and look out.

Long shot facing Wyatt as he continues to come down the street.

Long shot from the side of Ike and Phin. Ike takes his gun from his shoulder and looks over in the direction of Old Man Clanton.

Another long shot of Wyatt, still advancing. He carries his six-gun in his hand, but not in shooting position. This time he continues to come forward until he is out of the frame.

Return to the side shot of the Clantons.

CLANTON: Wait till they get closer, ya fools!

Long shot of Wyatt, now walking close to part of a corral. He enters a corral gate.
   Long shot of Wyatt seen moving behind a lattice of wooden fence; horses move in the background. Wyatt stops behind the fence, his face framed by its vertical poles.
   Long shot over a fence into an open area, where an unused stagecoach sits. Doc comes past the camera and quietly crosses over the fence, heading toward a building at the end of the fence and near the stagecoach. Morgan follows him.
   Long shot into the entrance of the yard with the stagecoach. At the back is the carriage house that Doc and Morgan have been moving toward. They become visible crossing in front of the open door of the carriage house and halting behind the empty stagecoach.
   Medium shot of Wyatt, who has not moved, but is watching Doc and Morgan. He takes his hat off as a signal.
   Return to long shot of the yard with the stagecoach. Doc and Morgan look toward the camera. They see Wyatt's signal, go into the carriage house, and open its back door. One man can be seen creeping along the far side of a fence to the left of the carriage house; the other is still framed in the back doorway.
   Medium shot of Wyatt. He puts his hat back on his head.
   Return to the long shot of the stagecoach yard. The second figure now leaves the doorway and moves stealthily along behind the fence.
   Medium shot of Wyatt, still looking out over the fence. He now moves slowly out of the frame.
   Long shot of Old Man Clanton. He moves along the rail to join Ike and Phin.

CLANTON: Phin, cover your brother.

Phin crosses behind the other two. As camera pans to follow him, he vaults over one fence and disappears. Old Man Clanton moves back to his original position, so that he is on the right side of the entrance gate. Ike, now out of the shot, remains on the left.

Long shot from behind Wyatt, who is moving behind the ends of a series of covered wagons.

Medium shot of Phin and Sam Clanton. Sam cocks his gun and fires.

Long shot of Wyatt between two wagons; he dives behind a hillock as Sam's shot is heard.

Long shot of Doc and Morgan. Hearing the shot, they jump into a ditch for cover.

Long shot looking along the side of one of the wagons. Wyatt is now moving toward the far end of the wagon, using the side for cover.

Long shot of Doc and Morgan crouching in the ditch. The sound of horses in the distance. Morgan pulls at Doc's shirt and points ahead of him.

Long shot of a stagecoach moving rapidly in open country. The camera pans to follow the stagecoach.

Long shot of the ditch again. Doc crawls out followed by Morgan.

Return to the long shot from the side of the wagon. Wyatt is still standing at the side close to the front end. Ahead of him, across the road and behind the corral, the stagecoach can be seen in the distance.

Long shot looking across the front of the covered wagon toward the corner behind which Wyatt is concealed. His hand appears and grabs onto the rim of the protruding front wheel.[37]

WYATT *(still not visible)*: Mornin', Mr. Clanton.

Long shot of the entrance gate to the O.K. Corral. At the sound of Wyatt's voice, Clanton and Ike are surprised. They tense themselves and raise their guns.
    Return to previous shot. Wyatt emerges from behind the wagon. He holds his gun chest high, but by its barrel, so that it is clear he does not intend to shoot. He moves around the wheel and stands in front of the wagon, putting one foot up on the wagon tongue.

WYATT: Let's talk awhile.

Medium shot of Ike Clanton, who quickly pulls his rifle up and aims it at Wyatt.

CLANTON *(off-screen) (sharply)*: Ike!

Long shot of the entrance to the O.K. Corral. Clanton and Ike stand there. Old Man Clanton puts his foot up on a bottom rail, but still keeps his gun pointed at Earp.

CLANTON: Well, now, you go right ahead and talk.
WYATT (LS): I got a warrant here for you and your sons, chargin' the murder of James and Virgil Earp. There's also a charge of cattle rustlin'. *(Medium low angle shot of Clanton with his gun pointed.)* I'm givin' you a chance to submit to proper authority.
CLANTON: Well, you come on right in here, Marshal, and serve your warrant.
WYATT (MS): Which one of you killed James?
CLANTON (MS): I did, and the other one too.

Long shot of the gate of the corral. Ike kicks it open and begins to walk out, gun at the ready, with his father dropping back to cover him. The sound of the stagecoach has grown much louder.

IKE: And I'm gonna kill you.

Long shot from behind Ike. Across the road two covered wagons stand, with Wyatt next to the farther one. As Ike advances, the stagecoach rushes by, raising a cloud of dust that obliterates the other side of the road. Ike moves up his side of the road, away from the camera and nearer the point where Wyatt had been seen. Suddenly two shots are heard, and Ike falls to the ground. Wyatt can barely be seen through the dust.

Long shot from behind Doc as he climbs over a fence into a corral full of horses.

Medium shot of Doc from the front just as he has lifted his upper body above the top rail. He begins to cough and pulls out his handkerchief, lowering his face into it.

Long shot of Phin and Sam, behind a corral rail. Both hear the cough, pivot, and begin firing.

Return to the medium shot of Doc, who doubles over clutching his chest.

Long shot from behind Doc as he falls backward off the fence to the ground. Morgan is behind Doc; he steps around Doc and goes up to the rail.

Long shot of Morgan behind the railing. A horse passes in front of him, blocking him off for a moment. As the horse disappears, Morgan begins to fire.

Long shot across the horses milling in the corral. On the far side, Phin and Sam fire back at Morgan.

Return to the previous shot, with Morgan firing and horses milling about in the foreground.

Again, a long shot toward Phin and Sam, but they are obscured by milling horses in the foreground.

Long shot of an open area seen through horizontal rail bars. Wyatt runs across the frame from left to right, firing as he runs. The camera pans slightly to the left as Sam Clanton lurches into the frame from the left, on this side of the fence. His gun falls from his hand as he topples face up on the ground next to a horse trough filled with water. The camera pans down to follow his fall. Gunshots splatter the water in the trough.

Long shot of Phin. He is balanced on the top of the railing of the corral with the milling horses in front of him. He takes off his hat, jumps in among the horses, and slowly advances toward the camera, firing with one hand and waving his hat in front of him with the other. Horses keep crossing the frame in front of him. Phin keeps moving forward until he reaches a wooden post in the middle of the corral.

Medium shot of Doc, his head framed by two horizontal rails. He is using the rails to support the upper part of his body. One hand on the upper rail holds his handkerchief, the other steadies his gun on the lower rail. He fires.

Long shot of Phin, who staggers and falls next to the post.

Return to the shot of Doc, whose head drops and slides down out of the frame. His handkerchief, looped over the rail, flutters in the wind.

Long shot of a corner of the corral house. Clanton, firing, retreats inside through a door on the left. Wyatt enters from the foreground and runs diagonally across the frame, flattening himself out against the wall of the house on the far right, next to a window.

WYATT: Throw your gun down and come on out, old man.

A rifle is tossed through the door. Clanton follows, with his hands raised. He turns and lurches toward the camera, looking dazed. Wyatt comes along the side wall from the window and stands next to Clanton, slightly behind him.

CLANTON (*looking ahead of him, not at Wyatt*): My boys! (*calling them*) Ike! Sam! Phin! Billy!
WYATT: They're dead. (*bitterly, his voice rising*) I ain't gonna kill you. I hope you live a hundred years, feel just a little what my Pa is going to feel. Now get out o' town. Start wanderin'.

Shakily, his hands still raised, Clanton goes to his horse and mounts, as the camera pans with him.
　　Medium shot of Morgan straddling a top rail, still with his gun out, held at rest in front of him.
　　Long shot of Clanton turning his horse.
　　Return to the shot of Morgan, now adjusting the chamber of his gun.

Long shot of Clanton from behind as he rides out through the main gate of the corral, with the road and the town ahead of him. When his horse has gone a few paces beyond the gate, Clanton turns in the saddle and draws a gun.
   Return to the shot of Morgan who, fanning his gun, fires three quick shots.
   Return to shot of Clanton. He slumps on his horse and then falls to the ground.[38]
   Return to shot of Morgan, his gun still pointed, staring out toward Clanton. Wyatt comes to stand at the rail next to Morgan, his back to the camera.

MORGAN: Wyatt . . .
WYATT: Doc?
MORGAN: Yeah. *(He swings his leg over to the far side of the rail, drops down, and begins to walk away from the camera.)*

Wyatt climbs over the rail and also disappears, as camera tilts slightly up toward the sky.
   Long shot from behind the rail where Doc fell; Wyatt and Morgan stand on the far side, facing the camera and looking down at Doc's body.[39]
   Medium shot as Morgan looks at Wyatt, and Wyatt continues to look at Doc.
   Return to previous long shot. Wyatt carefully steps around the body and moves out of the frame near the camera as the scene fades out.

Long establishing shot of the road heading out of Tombstone into open country. The land ahead is flat with a huge mesa in the center distance. No buildings are visible, only some fencing running along the right side of the road. Clementine stands by the fence on the right. A wagon and a horseman come into the frame from the lower right, heading out of town. They pull to a stop as they reach Clementine.
   Medium shot of Clementine near the fence.
   Medium shot of Morgan at the reins of the buggy, seen from behind.

MORGAN *(tipping his hat)*: Good-bye, ma'am. Mighty nice to have made your acquaintance. *(He turns to the horses.)* Git along, horses. *(The wagon begins to move out of the frame.)*

Medium shot of Wyatt on horseback. He dismounts as the sounds of the wagon moving down the road are heard.
   Long shot looking down the road. Wyatt crosses to where Clementine is standing.
   Medium shot of Clementine. Wyatt enters the shot on the right. They stand facing one another.

CLEMENTINE: There're so many things I wanted to say and . . . now nothing seems appropriate.

WYATT: Yes, ma'am, I . . . Yeah, I know. *(pause)* The Mayor says you might be stayin' here a while, maybe helpin' get a school started.

CLEMENTINE: Yes. I'm the new schoolmarm.

WYATT: That's mighty nice, ma'am. Me and Morg are goin' out to see Pa, tell him what happened. I might come East again, get some cattle, maybe stop by here again.

CLEMENTINE *(with a touch of eagerness)*: Stop by the schoolhouse?

Medium shot of Wyatt from behind Clementine.

WYATT: Yes, ma'am, I sure will. *(He hesitates, then bends over, and kisses her gently on the cheek.)* Good-bye, ma'am.

Return to the medium shot of the two facing each other. Wyatt shakes her hand.

CLEMENTINE: Good-bye. *(Wyatt turns and leaves the frame.)*

Long shot of Wyatt mounting his horse. Mounted, he looks toward Clementine and begins to smile.

WYATT: Ma'am, I sure like that name . . . Clementine. *(He raises his hat in a salute.)*

Long shot of the road, with Morgan's wagon a small mark in the distance. Wyatt spurs his horse down the road, as Clementine stands in the road watching him. "My Darling Clementine" begins to be sung on the soundtrack, gradually growing louder.

Long shot of Clementine in the road walking slowly toward the camera, still looking after Wyatt. She stops, but continues to look after him.

Long shot of the road from above and behind Clementine. She continues watching Wyatt, who is now a small figure on the road and is rapidly catching up with the wagon.

Fade out.

Notes on the
Shooting Script

1. In the shooting script (hereafter SS), after the brothers are introduced visually, the first dialogue is an exchange among the four of them, as they debate whether to make camp or to push on. The scene suggests some minor friction among the brothers, and it also introduces a more talkative Wyatt:

    WYATT
    Someday Morg might take a notion to call you on one of your empty dares, Virg, and then where'll you be at? The way I figger it, there's nothin' more embarrassin' than for a man to be left sprawled out— smack in the middle of an empty dare.

2. In SS, the two Clantons ride up to the Earp brothers, and all the brothers except James participate in the conversation. The sense of potential conflict with the Clantons is made very clear, and Old Man Clanton is forced to "back down under the granite stares of the Earp brothers."

3. Both Wyatt and Morgan offer to stay with James in SS. At first Wyatt has no strong desire to go to town but is persuaded by Morgan and Virgil.

4. As the Earps enter Tombstone, the SS portrays a more turbulent town than the film depicts:

    Morgan, Wyatt, and Virgil glance around interestedly as they move down the street. From the honky-tonks come the sound of tinny pianos. They continue on, taking everything in. They swerve their horses to avoid a group of mounted cowhands who come whooping down the street, guns out, shooting into the air in what passes in Tombstone for youthful exuberance. Steadying their horses, they proceed on down the street. Suddenly the door of a chop house bursts open and a white-coated Chinaman hurtles out, followed by several noisy cowhands. As the Chink flees across the street, one of the cowhands shoots a pattern about his feet. The cowhands roar with laughter and re-enter the chop house.

5. During the SS scene in the barber shop, Virgil reads a piece from the local newspaper recording the latest death by shooting. After Indian Charlie's shots have smashed the mirror, the scene ends with the barber crawling on his hands and knees out the rear door and Wyatt and his brothers seeking cover on the floor.

6. The SS version of this scene gives Kate Nelson a prominent role. She is clearly the local madam, with her brothel called Kate Nelson's Boarding House. Here she and her ladies are all huddled on the roof of the house, escaping Indian Charlie. From the roof Kate shouts down demands for "proper police pertection" to the Mayor and the Marshal. Wyatt, on the other hand, does not appear in the scene at all until after he has subdued the Indian. The townspeople in the street hear a thud, and Wyatt then appears through the boarding house door, dragging the Indian behind him, as in the film.

7. After discovering James's body and protecting it with a slicker, the brothers talk briefly about how to tell Pa and Nancy (Cory Sue's name in SS) and about whether they can pick up the killers' trail.

8. In his meeting with Wyatt in the lobby, Clanton attempts a convivial tone in SS. "Well, if you need any help, call on us. Us cattlemen gotta stick together. Come and take a whiskey." The conclusion of the scene also differs: "As Wyatt exits we leave the Clantons looking after him soberly and thoughtfully. Ike, his rifle at ready, walks to the door and stands there looking ominously into the dark street."

9. This scene is the first in which we see Tombstone by daylight. SS describes it "with all the frantic hustle and bustle of a boom town mushrooming out of the desert":

The street is jammed with activity. New frame one-story business buildings are being hammered together in gaps left between bars and honky-
tonks. Covered wagons—some drawn by horses, others by oxen—laden
with families and their household effects lumber through the busy town.

The conversation among the brothers refers to their duties as peace officers,
but makes no mention of any efforts to find the rustlers.

10. Here the SS includes a brief scene in which the theater owner asks Wyatt
to attend the performance that night and keep an eye on things. "Last week
one of the miners shot the villain right in the middle of the second act. Had
to go on and do my bird imitations."
    The SS also differs in that a comic sequence involving Granville Thorn-
dyke, the drunken actor, is omitted in the film. He is discovered asleep in
the stagecoach, an empty whiskey bottle at his side. He was expected to
arrive with a company, but they have run out on him. The theater owner
tells him what disappointed audiences are likely to do. Thorndyke has as
one of his props a skull which he keeps mislaying (hence his nickname
"Yorick" in the film).

11. In SS, there is a stage with a curtain at the end of the saloon, and Chihuahua,
introduced as "the Sweetheart of the Southwest," is more formally an
entertainer than in the film. Men at the bar ogle her and Billy Clanton tries
to get her to sit on his lap. Here, she is more flirtatious and venal than in
the film. She steals a bag of money from a miner's pocket. In the scene that
follows, omitted in the film, Chihuahua goes to her room to hide the stolen
money and Billy Clanton is waiting for her. He threatens to tell the Marshal
about the stolen money unless she takes up with him and boasts that he is
more of a man than Doc. Chihuahua pretends to give in and allows Billy to
kiss her. He promises to return the next night.

12. In SS, Doc pulls out a silk handkerchief, holds it by a corner, and offers
the other end to the gambler, saying "Take it and draw." He repeats the
gesture when he challenges Wyatt later in the scene. As the gambler leaves,
Doc fires behind him into the wall and then roars with laughter.

13. Morgan and Virgil do not join Wyatt and Doc for a drink in the SS scene.
Instead, Doc tells Wyatt he wished they could have had the "draw," be-

cause it would have meant risk. Wyatt finds it more sensible to shoot at beer bottles.

14. When Doc and Wyatt leave the theater, the SS scene continues in Doc's box. Billy pulls Chihuahua behind the curtains, kisses her, and gives her a pearl necklace. That scene is followed by another, also not in the film, in which Doc and Wyatt are on their way to get Thorndyke. Doc admits that Chihuahua is a "two-timing little coquette"; then he grins and adds, "But she'll look beautiful at my funeral." Wyatt says he is beginning to understand Doc.

15. In SS, Billy is not present in this scene, but Old Man Clanton is there throughout. The scene ends after Wyatt's departure with Sam and Phin about to draw their guns, until Old Man Clanton says, "Sit down. I'll settle it in my own way and in my own good time."

16. A brief scene appears in SS in which Wyatt sends Thorndyke off to the theater and then goes to find Doc at the Oriental. Doc quotes Shakespeare again, while Wyatt acknowledges: "First time I heard it. Parts I could understand makes a powerful lot of sense—especially that last about conscience makin' cowards out of all of us."

   Another omitted scene follows. Thorndyke is in the bar the next day reading about his performance, which he was too drunk to remember, in the local paper. The skull, missing again, is brought in by Kate Nelson.

17. Wyatt's meeting with the gambler(s) is presented differently in SS and placed much earlier in the narrative—just after the scene in front of the jail with Morgan and Virgil. There are two gamblers, who pretend to be salesmen of men's furnishings. Wyatt kicks open their suitcase, and gambling equipment spills out. Wyatt orders the men back into the stagecoach and, frightened, they comply.

18. The scene in Doc's bedroom is not in SS. Instead, Wyatt leaves the bags in Clementine's bedroom and, as he leaves, "looks at Clementine an unbearably long time—his eyes full of pathos and yearning. Then in a quiet voice: 'I like the name Clementine, Ma'am.'" Clementine then takes out a picture of herself and Doc, with the inscription "To the future Mrs. John Holliday—with love."

19. The SS introduces this scene with a prologue at the kitchen table in which François, the chef, identified as the former salad chef for the Emperor Maximilian of Mexico, prepares coleslaw and hovers over Doc as he is about to apply the dressing. The scene makes use of comic contrasts between François's expectations of elegant table behavior and Wyatt's incomprehension.

As a result of this prologue, SS shifts the vantage point for the arrival of Clementine: in the film, we are with her prior to the meeting with Doc; in SS, we are with him.

20. In SS, the scene on the back porch ends at this point, and Doc escorts Clementine back to the hotel. As they walk, she reminds him of how he saved the life of a boy in Boston because the boy had the will to live. They pass the boarding house, where one of the girls calls to Doc about Chihuahua; Clementine is simply amused. The scene between Clementine and Doc ends in the Mansion House lobby:

CLEMENTINE (quietly emotional)
You've become a coward, John. You're running away from life. Your illness has made you terrified and frightened of it. A silly notion of self-sacrifice—of not wanting to hurt people who love you—salves your conscience—and makes you think that what you're doing is right. It isn't. I'm only one of those people who love you, John. There is your mother—your sister—a world of friends. I came for them as well as for myself. Surely you don't think that "I'm sorry, Clem" will do as an answer. It may for them—but not for me.

DOC
Quite a speech. Are you finished?

CLEM (quietly)
Yes.

DOC
Then I'll make one. Short and final. Doctor John Holliday is dead. Everything was buried with him. His love for his mother—his sister—his world of friends—yes, even his love for Clementine Carter. And as for his epitaph—you've chosen an appropriate one—coward.

21. The scene with Doc alone in his bedroom is not in SS.

22. The barber shop scene is not in SS.

23. Although this scene exists in SS, Chihuahua's tossing the milk at Morgan and Wyatt's balancing act were added during the filming. Chihuahua is carrying the pitcher because, in SS, Doc on occasion orders milk at the bar because of his illness.

24. This scene occurs later in SS, after the Sunday church meeting and after a scene where Clementine visits James's grave (omitted in the film).

25. What follows is the entire church meeting sequence, in the SS version.

EXT. MANSION HOUSE—PORCH
Clementine and Wyatt look on. She has caught the spirit of the activity.

> CLEMENTINE
> A church comes to Tombstone. I think it's thrilling. Would you mind if I went along, Mr. Earp?

> WYATT (off balance)
> Well—

> CLEMENTINE
> You were going, weren't you?

> WYATT
> Yes—yes, ma'am?

> CLEMENTINE
> Shall we go?

Clementine takes Wyatt's arm. Camera follows them as they walk by Kate Nelson's Boarding House. From the windows, Kate and some of her "ladies" are looking out.

> KATE (with affected dignity)
> Good morning, Marshal.

> WYATT
> Howdy, Mrs. Nelson. (covering up to Clementine)
> A—a ladies' boardin' house.

CLEMENTINE (with a smile)
Yes, I know. We have them in Boston too.

Both laugh. Actually, it's the first time we have seen Wyatt happy. They walk along in silence for a while.

CLEMENTINE
I saw you bring John back last night.

WYATT
Yeah . . .

CLEMENTINE
I looked in on him after you left.
There was a blood spot on his pillow.
Was he in a fight?

WYATT
He'll be all right, ma'am.

CLEMENTINE (worried)
Will he?

Wyatt observes her concern—but says nothing.

They come up to a skeleton of the church building. The only thing completed is the floor and some studding that supports the bell tower. There is considerable activity about the church as a cross-section of Tombstone's citizens gather for their first service. Simpson is pulling on the bell rope with determination.

SIMPSON (his face aglow)
You come after all, Marshal! Fine!
Fine! Good mornin', young lady.
We'll get this dad-blasted meetin'
under way in a jiffy.

Wyatt and Clementine are amused by Simpson's earthiness.

SIMPSON (stops pulling the rope)
Step into the Lord's house, folks!
It ain't a fittin' place for Him yet
—but by the cherubim, it will be.

(to an elderly couple)
Mornin', Tom—Mrs. Evans.

MRS. EVANS
Good mornin'. What's this I hear from Marsha Goodwin about us havin' dancin' after the service. In a church, too. Ain't proper—is it, Mr. Simpson?

SIMPSON
Ain't proper? Mrs. Evans—I've read the Good Book from cover to cover and back again and I nary found one word agin it. The Lord don't care *how* you praise Him—*when* you praise Him or *where* you praise Him—just so long as you keep on praisin' Him. Inside folks— inside.

As Wyatt, Clementine, the Evans couple enter followed by Simpson, we

DISSOLVE:

ABOUT FIFTY PEOPLE—MEN, WOMEN AND CHILDREN
are seated on makeshift benches, chairs and wooden sawhorses. Simpson is up front before the "pulpit" which is an improvised and contrived easel on a soap box. He holds a prayer book in his hands and a fiddle tucked under his arm. Behind him are two flags. One is the American flag (38 stars in 1880) and the other is the flag of the Territory of Arizona.

SIMPSON
Until we git a reg'lar church parson, I take it on myself to pass the Lord's word along—hopin' and prayin' He'll forgive me for it. We'll commence by singin' "Shall We Gather At The River."
(with true pride)
The first congregation of the Protestant Church of Tombstone will please rise.

The congregation rises and Simpson leads them in singing the above-mentioned hymn.

During the above, camera has panned and covered all principals present. Among them is Old Man Clanton (without his sons) and the Town Drunk. When the prayer is concluded, Simpson indicates for everyone to sit.

SIMPSON
The Good Book says: "Thou art Peter, and upon this rock I will build
my church; and the gates of hell shall not prevail agin it." And I say
to you, Lord, that *nobody*—none of them likkered-up galoots over
to the Oriental or Silver Strike Saloon—none of them rustlers—
outlaws—hurray boys—nor Kate Nelson and her dancin' hall gals,
can stop Your word from bein' heard in Tombstone. Now that we got
Wyatt Earp and his brothers keepin' the peace, Lord—Your word and
the law will march together. We're gainin' on 'em all the time, Lord.
We got a good holt of the devil and by the cherubim, we won't let
go. And now, Lord, we ask Your blessing on this here church we're
buildin', and in Your name—I give thanks for the donations and
offerings we are about to collect.

Get goin', Tom—Jess. Pass the hats. Refreshments and dancin' will
now commence.

So saying, Simpson steps down from the pulpit and starts playing. Other
musicians join in. A few of the men pass their top hats around . . .
others begin talking in groups . . . dancing.

INT. CHURCH—WYATT—CLEMENTINE

CLEMENTINE (spiritually impressed)
I won't forget this for a long time. Thank you, Mr. Earp, for bringing me.

WYATT (smiles)
It's the other way around. Truth is I wasn't comin'. Mighty glad I did
though.

Evans comes into shot with the collection hat. Wyatt and Clementine
each drop in a silver dollar.

EVANS
Much obliged, folks.

Evans exits.

CLEMENTINE
If you have the time, Mr. Earp—I'd like to stay for the dancing.

WYATT
I've got plenty of time—but I'm not much of a hand at dancin'.

CLEMENTINE
Nonsense. You're probably a polished dancer.

WYATT
No, ma'am. And you can take my word for it.

INT. CHURCH—CLOSE SHOT

Wyatt and Clementine are dancing. (To the music of three fiddlers) Wyatt—decidedly no Massine—is giving his all.

WYATT
Can't say I didn' warn you.

CLEMENTINE (smilingly)
What you may lack in polish, you make up in zeal—Mr. Earp.

Camera pulls back to a full shot revealing that the church floor has been cleared of the benches and chairs, etc. Some of the citizens, including Simpson and his wife, are dancing—others on the fringes—are having refreshments and visiting. In the b.g. Morgan and Virgil enter.

INT. CHURCH—MED. SHOT

Virgil and Morgan look off and are surprised to see Wyatt here.

VIRGIL
That lyin' son-of-a-prairie dog.

MORGAN (primping)
Can't blame him none—with a ladies' man like me around.

VIRGIL
She sure is pretty.

MORGAN
Sure is. Reminds me some of Nancy.

INT. CHURCH—ANOTHER ANGLE

The music stops. Wyatt and Clementine finish with a flourish.

CLEMENTINE
Thank you, Mr. Earp.

WYATT
My pleasure, ma'am.

Virgil and Morgan enter shot.

WYATT
Howdy. My brothers. Morgan and Virgil. Miss Carter.

CLEMENTINE
How do you do?

MORGAN
Howdy.

VIRGIL (the cavalier)
Pleased to meet you, Miss Carter.

The music starts again.

VIRGIL
Would you like dancin' this piece with me, ma'am?

CLEMENTINE
I'd be delighted.

VIRGIL
Step aside, men, and watch an old hand cut loose.

Virgil and Clementine dance away. Wyatt and Morgan watch them for a minute.

MORGAN
Daw-gone—if that kid ain't a stepper. Takes after Pa.

WYATT
I don't.

Old Man Clanton eases into shot.

OLD MAN CLANTON
Good mornin', sons.

WYATT
G'mornin'.

Morgan nods.

OLD MAN CLANTON
Nice party.

WYATT
Fine.

OLD MAN CLANTON
Been meaning to ask you. Find out anymore who rustled your cattle?

WYATT
Got a pretty fair idea.

OLD MAN CLANTON
That's so? *Good*. Maybe this town'll turn out like Simpson said—honest and God-fearin'. When you figgerin' on roundin' up these rustlers?

WYATT
Haven't made up my mind yet.

OLD MAN CLANTON
Got a big shipment to make next week. Be safer to wait until you've got 'em cooped up. You think so?

WYATT
It would.

OLD MAN CLANTON
You couldn't be giving me an idea just about when you—

WYATT
It won't be long, Mr. Clanton—and I promise you, you'll be one of the first to know.

OLD MAN CLANTON
Much obliged.

Old Man Clanton shuffles out of shot.

MORGAN (quietly)
What *are* you waitin' for, Wyatt? I'd bet my right eye that swamp-crook and his sons were mixed up in it. I got an *annoyin' feelin'* about it.

WYATT
Maybe. But you can't hang a man on an annoyin' feelin'.

INT. CHURCH—DANCE FLOOR

Virgil and Clementine are dancing nicely together.

INT. CHURCH—FRINGE OF CROWD

A group of people are around a punch bowl. Among them the Town Drunk. A lady offers him a glass of punch. He tastes it—swallows it with difficulty—then surreptitiously sets it down on the table—shakes his head and exits sadly from the building.

INT. CHURCH—ANOTHER ANGLE

Kate Nelson, dressed conservatively, enters. She remains standing there—uncertainty written on her face. Simpson comes over to her.

SIMPSON
Good mornin', Kate.

KATE
Good mornin', Mr. Simpson. (holds out a leather pouch)
I—I—brought you some money if—if you don't mind takin' it from me.

SIMPSON
Mind? I should say not. That'll be payin' Jacob back for what Esau done to him.
(grabs the pouch)

KATE
I'm much obliged to you.

SIMPSON
Look here, Kate. Not over an hour ago—I got through cussin' you out

to the Lord—and I'm gonna keep a-doing' it. But by the cherubim and the seraphim, when you're in His House, you're welcome.

KATE
Mighty kind of you, Mr. Simpson.

SIMPSON
The *Lord's* kind . . . when you get to know Him better. Step in and join the folks.

Simpson exits.

INT. CHURCH—ANOTHER ANGLE

Kate is a pathetic creature as she stands there—not knowing whether to come farther or leave. Wyatt sees her and goes up to her.

WYATT
Risk a dance with me, Mrs. Nelson?

KATE
Reckon—it be the other way around. If you're gambler enough . . .

Wyatt puts his arm about Kate and they dance away.

INT. CHURCH—CLOSE SHOT—VIRGIL—CLEMENTINE

Clementine notices Wyatt dancing with Kate.

CLEMENTINE
Isn't that Mrs. Nelson?

Virgil gives a quick "take" not unnoticed by Clementine who smiles mischievously.

VIRGIL
Yes—yes—I think so. How—do *you* know her?

CLEMENTINE
Doesn't everyone? She was even mentioned from the pulpit today.

VIRGIL
Darned if I can figger Wyatt out. But you can be sure, ma'am—he don't do nothin' unless he's got a good purpose.

CLEMENTINE
I'm sure of that, Mr. Earp. No *gentleman* does.

INT. CHURCH—WYATT—KATE

They are dancing. Kate is heated and puffing.

KATE
I'm for quittin'—if you are.

They stop.

KATE
Whew! The spirit's willin'—but the flesh ain't.

They walk to the sidelines.

KATE
Much obliged, Mr. Earp. Guess I'll be going. So long—and—bless you, son.

WYATT
So long.

Kate exits. Wyatt walks back to Morgan.

MORGAN
You took after Pa *then*.

Wyatt acknowledges Morgan's compliment with a brotherly look. The music has stopped. Virgil and Clementine enter shot—both are smiling.

CLEMENTINE (with a western twang)
He's *sure* an old hand and he *sure* did cut loose.

Everyone smiles.

CLEMENTINE (to Morgan)
Now—what about you?

MORGAN
No—I thank you. I—I've got to get along. Come on, Virg. Excuse us, ma'am.

VIRGIL
But the dance—

MORGAN
We got work to do. Come on.

Morgan practically pulls Virgil away with him—leaving Clementine and Wyatt amused.

CLEMENTINE
They're nice. I like the Earp brothers. Are there more?

WYATT
No, ma'am. There were—up until a while back.

CLEMENTINE
What do you mean, Mr. Earp?

WYATT
The youngest, James, was killed by rustlers.

CLEMENTINE
I'm terribly sorry.

WYATT
He's buried out in the valley—not far from here. Planned on goin' out there. Pretty nice ride—if you'd like to come, ma'am.

CLEMENTINE
I'd very much like to. I'll be back in time for the stage, won't I?

WYATT
Won't take but an hour or so. We can fetch a wagon over to the O.K. Corral.

CLEMENTINE
Then let's do it.

26. A scene, omitted in the film, in which Clementine visits James's grave with Wyatt. She breaks down and cries and then admits how much help Wyatt has been to her. Wyatt urges her not to give up, but to stay and try to help Doc. "If you don't, Doc's washed up." They ride back through the valley and Clementine is deeply impressed by the landscape. "The wonder and power of it all! And yet so melancholy and lonely." Wyatt begins to hum "My Darling Clementine" and tells her that James used to sing it all the time.

27. This scene follows SS, except that, after Doc leaves the dining room, Clementine breaks into tears and rushes upstairs.

28. SS has, at this point, two brief scenes that are not in the film. In the first, Doc goes to the Wells Fargo office and forces the man who is riding shot-gun off the stage, taking his place. In the second, Billy comes looking for Chihuahua in the saloon, but gets a cool reception from her. The man whom Doc forced off the stage comes in, and Chihuahua overhears him talking about Doc riding off on the stage. She leaves the saloon, and the next scene begins in Clementine's room at the Mansion House.

29. In SS, Chihuahua begins to toss Clementine's belongings into her suitcase. "A knock-down drag-out fight commences." Downstairs, Wyatt is playing poker and hears the commotion. He rushes up and stops the fight. The cross has been torn off during the tussle, and Wyatt notices it as Chihuahua picks it up from the floor.

30. The scene continues in SS in order to reestablish the two men's friendship. Wyatt binds up Doc's flesh wound and gives him a drink from a jug on the stagecoach.

31. In SS, Chihuahua is shot before she identifies Billy.

32. In the film, the street is empty; in SS, a crowd gathers, and Billy has to fire a shot to disperse them so that he can ride off.

33. Clementine is part of this scene in SS; she, rather than Wyatt, convinces Doc that he must do the surgery. They speak after Chihuahua has been carried downstairs and they are left alone. "You've got to do it, John. You've no alternative. Not only is her life at stake . . . yours is too."

34. The remainder of the scene does not appear in SS. In its place Clementine and Doc speak together after the surgery. Clementine urges Doc to resume his earlier life, and Doc admits that he once again feels some pride in himself.

35. The Clantons leave the body of Virgil in the street without issuing any challenge in SS. The next scene begins in the office of the jail, with only Wyatt and Morgan present:

WYATT

We won't be goin' after 'em for a spell yet, Morg. Better sit.

MORGAN

Can't figure you sometime, Wyatt. Here you sit—calm—just like you was fixin' to go to a picnic—and all the time *my* blood's boilin' and racin'.

WYATT

That's why you better sit.

MORGAN

What makes you so cocksure they didn't pull out of here? More than likely they're in the next county by now.

WYATT

More than likely they're holed in somewhere waiting for us to come a-shootin'. Waitin' and worryin'.

MORGAN

Worryin'?

WYATT

Yep—worryin'. Worryin' and wonderin'. Same as you're doin'—only more of it. Somethin' about bein' on the wrong side of the fence that kinda increases worryin'. Pretty soon they get to passin' the jug around. More they'll drink—more they'll need. First thing you know, you got 'em at a disadvantage—and all you've done to get it—is sit and wait.

36. The men go barefooted in SS in order to move more quietly. Simpson offers a prayer before they all leave:

SIMPSON

It's pretty simple what's goin' on down here, Lord. You've seen these dad-blasted things go on afore—and likely as not, You'll see 'em again. On one side is rustlin', thievin' and killin'. On the other is law and order and justice. We figger that's our side, Lord, and we ask your help— same as You gave it to Joshua at Jericho; same as when You pulled David from under the paw of the bear and the paw of the lion; same as when You made the whale throw up Jonah. Give Your blessings to these boys, Lord—so they can smite our dad-blasted enemies and bring peace to our community forever. Amen.

37. The conversation between Wyatt and Clanton is not in SS, nor does Ike advance toward Wyatt from the corral. Instead, the fight begins when Doc and Morgan succeed in surprising the Clantons from behind. They shoot first, killing Phin. As the exchange continues, Morgan is wounded, then Doc, as he drags Morgan to cover. Doc kills Sam, but is then shot and killed by the Clantons. In the meantime, Wyatt kills Ike. Old Man Clanton keeps firing until he runs out of ammunition, then emerges to face Wyatt defiantly.

38. Old Man Clanton is not killed in SS; Wyatt sends him off alone and Clanton rides out into the valley.

39. As in the earlier scene of James's death, here in SS Wyatt and Morgan exchange some brief comments about Doc, while in the film they look at his body in silence.

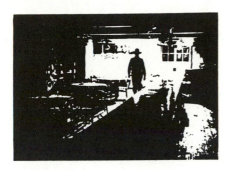

Interviews, Reviews, and Commentaries

Interviews

John Ford disliked discussing his own work and was notoriously uncommunicative when being interviewed. The 1964 article by Bill Libby, while not formally organized as an interview, is primarily given over to quoting Ford at great length. In it, Ford's comments about his favorite film genre are uncharacteristically expansive. The article contains Ford's most revealing statements about Western films and his reasons for making them.

Winston Miller, who is credited as co-writer with Samuel G. Engel of the script of *My Darling Clementine*, was an active Hollywood writer for nearly four decades. He wrote the screenplays for over thirty-five feature films between the 1930s and the mid 1960s, and he received three Screenwriters' Guild nominations for best screenplay. When he became a television producer, he stopped writing for films. He now lives in Beverly Hills, California. The interview with Miller in this volume took place in April 1982.

The Old Horseman Rides Again: John Ford Talks About Westerns

Bill Libby

When a motion picture is at its best, it is long on action and short on dialogue. When it tells its story and reveals its characters in a series of simple, beautiful, active pictures, and does it with as little talk as possible, then the motion picture medium is being used to its fullest advantage. I don't know any subject on earth better suited to such a presentation than a Western.

The people who coined that awful term "horse opera" are snobs. The critics are snobs. Now, I'm not one who hates all critics. There are many good ones and I pay attention to them and I've even acted on some of their suggestions. But most criticism has been destructive, full of inaccuracies and generalizations. Hell, I don't think the leading newspaper reviewers even go to see most of the Westerns. They send their second string assistants. And they're supposed to be very nasty and very funny in their reviews. Well,

From Bill Libby, "The Old Wrangler Rides Again," *Cosmopolitan* (March 1964):14–21.

it's a shame, because it makes it a crime to like a Western. But, there have been bad and dishonest romantic stories, too, and war stories, and people don't attack all romantic movies or war movies because of these. Each picture should be judged on its own merit. In general, Westerns have maintained as high a level as that of any other theme.

The critics always say we make Westerns because it's an easy way to make money. This is hogwash. They're not cheap or easy to make. They have to be done on location, which is damned hard work, the most expensive and most difficult form of moviemaking. It's true Westerns generally make money. What the hell's wrong with that? If there were more concern with what the public wants and less with what the critics want, Hollywood wouldn't be in the awful fix it's in right now. This is a business. If we can give the public what it wants, then it's a good business and makes money. The audience is happy and we're happy. What the hell's wrong with that?

. . . When I come back from making a Western on location, I feel a better man for it. I don't think some of the modern trash makes anyone feel better for having read or seen it.

I don't recall a Western which ever had to carry a "For Adults Only" sign. When you go to a movie today, you feel guilty, as though you were going to a striptease. It all runs in cycles. Tomorrow, someone will make a picture about a boy and a dog, and it'll make money and then everyone will start making boy-and-dog pictures again.

Actually, I'm certainly not against sex on the screen if it's done in the right way. Many Westerns have a gusty [*sic*] sort of sex. And I think I made the sexiest picture ever, *The Quiet Man*. Now this was all about a man trying to get a woman into bed, but that was all right, they were married, and it was essentially a moral situation, done with honesty, good taste, and humor. These things are all fundamental to a good Western, too. In a Western, you can make a strong picture which is reasonably adult, yet a man can still take his children to see it, which is the way it should be. After all, we're not in the burlesque business.

I know the term "morality play" has been applied to Westerns, but I won't go that far, nor be so high-toned about it, but I do feel they have a basically moral quality, and I applaud this and think it's the way it should be.

We use immoral characters. In *Stagecoach*, we had Claire Trevor playing a woman of easy virtue and Thomas Mitchell playing a drunken doctor. We don't deny that there are such persons; we just aren't out to

glorify them or build every story around them. Incidentally, these have become stock characters in Westerns, and maybe they've become what you call "clichés," but they weren't always clichés, and I keep trying to do things fresh or different, just as many others in this business do.

There are no more clichés in Westerns than in anything else, and this applies to our moral approach, too. I don't think I, nor anyone else, have always garbed my heroes in white and my villains in black and so forth. Good doesn't always triumph over evil. It doesn't in life and it doesn't in all Westerns. Usually it does, but I think this is the way it should be. I have depicted some sad and tragic and unjust things in my Westerns, as have others.

. . . The men of the West were like Will Rogers. They were rugged and imperfect men, but many were basically gentle, and most were basically moral and religious, like most people who live with the land.

They had their own language, but it was not profane. They had a warm, rugged, natural good humor. Strong people have always been able to laugh at their own hardships and discomforts. Soldiers do in wartime. The old cowboy did in the Old West. And today, in the hinterlands, in places like Montana and Wyoming, there are working cowboys, and they even carry guns, usually .30 Winchesters, though for protection against animals, such as coyotes, not to shoot each other.

We've studied the history of these cowboys, past and present, and we've had some true Western characters, such as Pardner Jones, serving as technical experts on our films. I think some of the personality things I've mentioned have been very well portrayed in our Western film heroes. These men are natural. They are themselves. They are rugged individualists. They live an outdoor life, and they don't have to *conform.*

I think one of the great attractions of the Western is that people like to identify themselves with these cowboys. We all have an escape complex. We all want to leave the troubles of our civilized world behind us. We envy those who can live the most natural way of life, with nature, bravely and simply. What was that character's name? Mitty, that's it. We're all Walter Mittys. We all picture ourselves doing heroic things. And there are worse heroes than the Westerners for us to have.

The Western heroes may be "larger than life," but so are many of our historical heroes, and we hate to dispel the public's illusions. If we cast handsome men and attractive women in semibiographical roles, portraying persons who were really homely, we are doing no worse than has always been done in movies. I myself am a pretty ugly fellow. The public wouldn't pay to see me on film.

It is probable that the Westerns have been most inaccurate in overglamorizing and overdramatizing the heroes and villains of the period, and in playing up the gunfights. We could do without such stock characters as the hero who leaps from two stories onto his horse, fires twenty shots at a time from his six-shooter and has a comical, bearded rascal for his sidekick. But again, these are generalizations which don't apply to all Westerns.

We have been charged with using too much violence, with too often achieving a good end through the unfortunate use of violent means, and this charge has merit, but, after all, those *were* violent times. I've tried not to overdo this and so have a lot of men who have turned out good Westerns. The very term "gunslinger" makes us cringe, and we try to hold shoot-downs to a minimum. But men did carry guns and did shoot at each other. There wasn't much law for a long while, after all.

It is wrong to make heroic the villainous characters, such as Billy the Kid, who were more ruthless and vicious than anyone can imagine today. However, it is true that much of the conversion to law and order was accomplished by reformed criminals, who got sheriff's jobs because of their strong reputations. Men like Wyatt Earp had real nerve. They didn't have to use their guns. They overpowered the opposition with their reputations and personalities. They faced them down. They were lucky. A .45 is the most inaccurate gun ever made. If you've handled one, you know. Pardner Jones told me if you put Wild Bill Hickok in a barn with a six-shooter, he couldn't have hit the wall.

It is equally wrong for the heroes to have been made out to be pure Sir Galahads in so many cases, which is nonsense. However, those were different times than we know today. Mere survival took something out of the ordinary, and the men who dominated the time *were* out of the ordinary, really big men.

. . . In general, I don't think there is any aspect of our history that has been as well or completely portrayed on the screen as the Old West.

. . . There have to be some compromises with historical fact and accuracy in all movies. The public will simply not accept certain things which seem strange to them, true as they may be. You cannot, for example, show a general heading into battle, riding a mule, wearing corduroys, and a pith helmet, and shielding himself from the sun with an umbrella, yet General Crook actually did that.

Most Westerners really dressed in simple, rugged clothing, and were often very dirty. You got dirty on the range, you know, and laundries and bathrooms were sometimes hard to come by. Some time ago we reached the point where they would let our characters get out of the elaborate dress that once passed in movies for cowboy clothes, and let us put John Wayne, for example, into a part without a coat and with suspenders showing, as in *The Horse Soldiers*.

Actually, the thing most accurately portrayed in the Western is the land. I think you can say that the real star of my Westerns has always been the land. I have always taken pride in the photography of my films, and the photography of Westerns in general has often been outstanding, yet rarely draws credit. It is as if the visual effect itself were not important, which would make no sense at all.

When I did *She Wore a Yellow Ribbon*, I tried to have the cameras photograph it as Remington would have sketched and painted it. It came out beautifully and was very successful in this respect, I think. When I did *The Searchers*, I used a Charles Russell motif. These were two of our greatest Western artists, of course.

Is there anything more beautiful than a long shot of a man riding a horse well, or a horse racing free across a plain? Is there anything wrong with people loving such beauty, whether they experience it personally, or absorb it through the medium of a movie? Fewer and fewer persons today are exposed to farm, open land, animals, nature. We bring the land to them. They escape to it through us. My favorite location is Monument Valley, which lies where Utah and Arizona merge. It has rivers, mountains, plains, desert, everything the land can offer. I feel at peace there. I have been all over the world, but I consider this the most complete, beautiful, and peaceful place on earth.

Interview with Winston Miller

Robert Lyons

Int.: How did you become involved with *My Darling Clementine*?

Miller: Howard Hawks had hired me to write the screenplay for a *Saturday Evening Post* novelette that he had bought called "The Phantom Filly" by George Agnew Chamberlain, a lovely story about trotting horses in Indiana. I wrote the screenplay, and then I went into the service and didn't think much about anything for the next three years while I was in the Marine Corps. During that time, Howard sold the script to Twentieth Century. They made the picture with Henry Hathaway directing it, calling it *Home in Indiana*, and it was well received. So that came out just at the end of the war. At the time I got my discharge, I had two weeks' terminal leave left to me, so I stayed in uniform because I got a special rate at the Coronado Hotel. My wife and infant daughter came down for two weeks of fairly inexpensive luxurious living. Meantime, my agent called and asked if I would like to go to work for Twentieth Century. I said not for two weeks, I was enjoying life on the town. He said, "That's too bad. It's a John Ford picture." I said,

"I'll be up tonight." So I drove up and we talked. Twentieth gave me the two weeks, and after that I went to work with Ford.

It was an unusual situation. I'd just gotten out of the marines, Ford had just gotten out of the navy, Henry Fonda had just gotten out of the navy, Victor Mature had just gotten out of the Coast Guard. It was the first picture after the war for everybody.

So John Ford and I sat around for five or six weeks kicking this thing around, trying to cook up a story. Twentieth had once made a picture based on Wyatt Earp, and everybody in town had taken a shot at Earp, one way and another. But we disregarded that; we just started from scratch and made up our story. It was interesting to me because Ford was even by then practically a legendary character, and I enjoyed working with him.

Int.: It's interesting, too, that with the exception of *Stagecoach*, Ford hadn't made a Western for twenty years.

Miller: This film was in the old classic mold. I enjoyed it because I knew Ford's style. I had seen everything he ever made. I knew that he liked lean dialogue, and that's the way I always liked to write.

Int.: Then Ford had a hand in planning the film? Were you collaborating with him at least in talking over what you were going to do?

Miller: Oh, yes. He was the boss. This was a John Ford production, no question about that. We'd meet every day and just sit around and talk, just the two of us in his small office.

Incidentally, there were several things about Ford that were interesting. One was that he absolutely refused to talk about his work. There was no way anyone could drag anything out of him.

Int.: Yes, I've read that about Ford in a number of places.

Miller: I remember once he called me to come over to his office. Mel Ferrer and Joe Ferrer were there, and they were there to sit at the foot of the master and talk about directing and motivation and all that. And Ford to avoid that had me come over because Mel and Joe and I had all gone to the same college—we had all gone to Princeton. So while they wanted to talk movies, Ford wanted to talk old college days and Maine Stein songs. They were so frustrated that they didn't get to talk for one minute about what made him a great director. But he just would not talk about it. If anybody tried to read motivations into his work, he'd just say, "No kidding! Is that so?" I have read things about *My Darling Clementine* where people read things into it that weren't there. I knew because I wrote it. What you saw was what you got. There was no tertiary motivations.

But Ford was a fascinating man because he played a cat-and-mouse game. Sooner or later he wanted to dominate you. He would try to maneuver you into an unfortunate position. He succeeded in doing that to me just once. There was a scene at the end of the picture where Victor Mature grabbed the stagecoach and was leaving town. We were in with Zanuck talking about that. Ford and I got along fine, never a cross word; I minded my manners with him, but I was doing my share. I contributed most of the story because that was all I had to think about, whereas he was thinking of a lot of other things, casting and so forth. We got to this scene and he wanted Victor Mature to have the stagecoach driver with him at the confrontation with Henry Fonda. I wanted him to get rid of the stagecoach driver so there would be just the two of them. We were arguing this point, or rather discussing it, and Ford and Zanuck asked me why I didn't want the driver there, and I made an unfortunate statement. I said, "Well, it will make the scene cluttered." That was an unfortunate word, because Ford hopped on it, and he did a ten-minute solo on didn't I think he was capable of directing three people in a scene.

Int.: Well, you reached a compromise, because the driver is still there, but he stays up on the stagecoach.

Miller: It wasn't a compromise, because Ford did it the way he wanted to. At the time I tried to explain that I wasn't saying he couldn't direct a scene with three people in it. But he put me on the defensive and that pleased him more than a salary raise.

On the other hand, I saw Zanuck play him like a flute one day. Zanuck suggested a piece of business and Ford said, "That's corny." Zanuck said, "Jack, with anybody else, it would be. But the way I see you do it . . ." and Ford bought it. It was things like that that made it fun.

Int.: Had the cast been chosen when you were developing the script with Ford, so that you would have specific actors in mind as you worked?

Miller: I'm afraid I don't remember, except that Fonda was set for it. Ford liked to work with him because Fonda's pace was Ford's pace. Ward Bond, I guess, was going to be in it because he was part of the stock company.

John Ford liked to hold on a person, like scenes in the bar where he just held on Fonda. He was one of the few actors you could do that with. Although his face didn't change, you knew he was thinking. And Ford liked

his walk. He liked to follow a man; he didn't like to pan the camera, he liked to keep it pretty stationary. And he could watch Fonda walk down a whole block. He had a unique walk. In other words, Fonda's style suited Ford's style.

Int.: Yes, Ford does that very often in *Clementine*. He simply lets Fonda walk away from the camera and creates a tremendous effect.

Miller: Ford didn't go in for any camera tricks at all. He was great for black and white; it was made for him. He liked that lean, stark effect.

Another reason I enjoyed working with him was he has this slant on people. He would sit there chewing his handkerchief, but he always saw things with that crazy Irish slant he had that I thought was wonderful. He was one of the few directors whose pictures you could see without screening the credits and say "This is a John Ford picture," because of his pacing and his attitude. But he loved a Western with his stock company, J. Farrell MacDonald, Ward Bond. . . .

Int.: And his brother, of course, was in many of them and was in *Clementine*.

Miller: He also loved something else. He did a picture called *Young Mr. Lincoln* with Fonda, in which there was a dance in which Fonda did his funny knee-high waltz. Well, Ford loved that, so we had that in *Clementine*. We wrote that church social scene so that Fonda could do his dance.

Int.: I remember in *Young Mr. Lincoln* another scene in which Fonda goes to the grave of Ann Rutledge and talks to her although she's gone. In *Clementine*, Fonda goes to his brother's grave and does much the same thing.

Miller: You know, that's funny. I was just checking over the script, because I hadn't looked at it in over thirty years, and I read that scene. I had assumed before we talked that I had thought of that, but now that you tell me about *Young Mr. Lincoln*, it was probably Ford's idea. You forget after thirty years, and you're willing to take credit for things you shouldn't.

One incident also might be of interest to you as an indication of how Ford operated, one that I've never forgotten. We were talking one day in his office. He thought in terms of scenes. He'd say he'd like to do a scene in a small Western town of a whore's funeral. Now the casket is being carried through the town on the way to the cemetery on a wagon, and only the madam and the girls are walking along behind it. As it passes the various stores, the town banker looks out and sees the caravan, and his conscience gets the better of him. You assume he was one of her customers. And finally his manhood asserts itself, and he goes out and falls in line behind the wagon. And one by one, all the men in the town go and fall in line. By the time it gets to the cemetery, it's a parade. This is the type of thing only Ford would think of.

Int.: Yes, it's both very funny and very moving at the same time.

Miller: Yes, it's got a lot of things going. But when we finished talking the whole thing out, he went about his other business and I went back to my own office and sat down and wrote the script. We would only meet occasionally, maybe not for two or three weeks. So I was writing away and one day I ran into him on the lot and we walked along together and he said "How's it coming?" I said, "Fine." He said, "How's the whore's funeral scene coming?" I said, "Jack, you know, I got to thinking about it and it just doesn't work because she wasn't a whore with a heart of gold." This was the part played by Linda Darnell.

Int.: I see. He wanted to use Chihuahua's death as the basis for that scene.

Miller: Yes, because in a way she was a whore in the town. I told Ford that she wasn't that kind of a girl. She was a mean no-good, and I went on at great length expounding why the scene wouldn't work. He didn't say a word; he just walked with his head down. Then when I got through, he said, "Well, I don't know what you're writing, but on the screen it's going to look a hell of a lot like a whore's funeral." That was the way he operated. He didn't put it in the picture because I was right. But it was going to be his decision, not mine.

Int.: In your script, you have a number of scenes that involve Jane Darwell as Kate Nelson, who runs the "boarding house" or brothel. I've read that much of the material was shot, but that then there were censorship problems. Do you recall such problems?

Miller: Well, you remember this was the late forties. To Ford, it was the town whorehouse, but in the script, it was her whatever you want to call it.

Int.: Ladies' boarding house.

Miller: But it was clear. But the Breen Office or the Hays Office* sent the usual admonishing memo, saying this is unacceptable. Ford dismissed that by sending a memo back saying, in

---

*Offices that enforced the motion picture industry's moral code from the 1920s to the 1960s.

effect, that it would be handled with John Ford's usual good taste. He didn't pay much attention to higher authority. As I remember that opening scene with the drunken Indian and the girls jumping out the windows—that pretty well indicated what it was.

Int.: But there were a couple of nice comic scenes involving Jane Darwell and the girls that were cut out, and there's a part of the dance at the church where Fonda dances with Darwell and that's also gone. At any event, in the finished film, Darwell's role has become so small that it's pretty clear that someone went to work with the scissors.

Miller: I saw Ford long after the picture was out and found that he was very displeased. Zanuck, who also prided himself on being a very good cutter, had cut behind Ford, which Ford didn't like at all. You know, Ford tried to shoot his pictures so that nobody could recut them. But Zanuck —who really was a good cutter, but not necessarily to Ford's liking—had decided that he wanted to make some changes and Ford was very unhappy about it. He felt it was no longer his picture. There was quite a sour note to it.

Int.: I notice that when Ford was interviewed in his late years and asked about his favorite films, he mentions different titles from one interview to another, but he never mentions *My Darling Clementine*. Do you think that is because he felt he had lost control over it?

Miller: Yes, and apparently that didn't happen to Ford often. As a matter of fact, he generally made a dictatorship look like a weak democracy as far as his authority was concerned.

Int.: Which was hard to achieve for a Hollywood director.

Miller: He achieved it with those Academy Awards. Then he established his own ground rules. One of the things that was fun in those days was sitting around the studio at the writers' table talking with members of the production staff who had worked with him and hearing John Ford stories. Some maybe were apocryphal, but most of them were true. In one of them he was called to see Zanuck. Zanuck was tied up with something, and Ford waited in his outer office for a while. After about twenty minutes he got up and said to Zanuck's secretary, "Tell Mr. Zanuck that John Ford has saved his money." He walked off the lot, got onto his boat, and went to Catalina. He was not a man to fool around with. If an actor was prone to trying to improve the script or add some new lines, Ford would create a

scene to embarrass him, so that from then on the guy would just do what he was told. Directors in those days each had some kind of a command personality, like a general, and this was Ford's.

They told another story where Ford was missing an angle in the dailies. The producer, I believe it was Arthur Hornblow, a man of some distinction in the business, was delegated to point it out to Ford, because nobody else wanted to. So he went down to the set, got Ford's attention, and just mentioned that it was a great scene and all that, but an angle seemed to be needed. Ford asked, "Do you think we really need it," and Hornblow said, "I think we do, Jack." Ford said "O.K., you shoot it," and walked off the set. Well, this helped to let a guy be left pretty much alone, which was all he ever wanted in the first place.

Int.: What was Samuel Engel's role in writing the film? [Engel was credited as producer and cowriter of the film.]

Miller: He came on the deal late. Ford and I had just about finished all our talks. I had known Sam Engel before, because when I was with Selznick, Selznick owned a book by Nevil Shute called *Ordeal*. He thought he would make it in England and have me write it and Sam Engel produce it. So I met Sam and we talked about it, and we picked out our accommodations on the *Queen Mary*. Then Selznick said that he just couldn't do anything else, it had to be *Gone With the Wind*. So I went on to other things and Sam left the studio. I didn't see him for years. Then he came back to Twentieth, where he had been before the war, and Zanuck put him on as the producer of *Clementine*. But much to my surprise I found that as I sent my scripts in—and as a courtesy I sent them to him first—he made changes. I brought this to his attention. I said, "Sam, I work alone. I don't collaborate, never have." He really had nothing to do on the picture. It was a John Ford production, and John Ford did not take kindly to anybody being called a producer. So when the whole thing was over, I went my way and everybody did, and Sam Engel put in for screen credit. I objected and we had a hearing before the Writers' Guild and he lost. A few weeks later it came up again, and he lost again. Then my wife and I took a trip, and Ford was off somewhere, and I came back and I got a notice that Engel's name was put on. I had asked Sam after the second hearing why he was so desirous of this line and he said, "Well, producer credit on a John Ford production means nothing." So I said, "Well, that's your hard luck, not mine." So after I saw this I called up and asked the guild what happened and was told that Engel had said he

was on location while it was being shot and made some additions. I was long gone from the picture then.

Int.: Then your work on the script was done before Ford began shooting the film.

Miller: Yes, I was finished before they started to shoot. I went on to some other studio and some other job. Sam stayed with it and on the basis of that they gave him a credit. By that time it was water under the bridge and I was sick and tired of the whole thing. The only time I ever had any unpleasantness with Ford was when I ran into him sometime later out at Lakeside Golf Club which we both belonged to, out at the practice tee, and he was very cool to me. I asked, "What's the matter?" He was sore that I hadn't called on him to appear at the hearing. I said, "Well, it wasn't your battle, it was mine." I didn't like it, but I had gone as far as I could. It actually resulted in changing the rules of the Writers' Guild whereby a man whose job is producer, whose title is producer (which means he technically can hire and fire you) cannot also be your collaborator without your prior consent. However, that's the way it happened. We never worked together on it. I hardly ever saw Sam Engel.

Int.: So it was really a collaboration between you and Ford.

Miller: Yes, we talked out every single scene, at least every basic scene. Basic things like the silver cross. We needed something, we didn't know what it was, to put Wyatt Earp on the Clantons' trail. Actually, if you analyze that picture, there were a lot of flaws in the construction. Earp stays in town to get his brother's killer, and we vamp for about sixty pages with what we hope are interesting scenes. We don't get back onto the brother's killer until way late in the script. Then there's that scene where he discovers the cross, and then we round third and head for home. But that was the way it seemed to evolve and Ford didn't care. Our theory was as long as it's interesting.

Int.: And the sense of Earp's getting involved with the town of Tombstone gets established in that middle section, too.

Miller: That was the meat of the picture. The reason he didn't do anything for so long about his brother's killer was because we couldn't think of anything for him to do.

Int.: Or you would be ending the picture.

Miller: The picture would have been over in two reels. So it was a question of just trying to say what would be interesting to have happen next. If I had known then that it was going to be sort of a semiclassic, at least in terms of how many reruns it's had on television, I might have been a little more protective of my credit.

Int.: One element in *Clementine* that you and Ford must have introduced was the conflict between the Earp family and the Clanton family. That isn't in *Frontier Marshal*, which is just a film about Wyatt Earp and Doc Holliday.

Miller: That was in the picture from the very beginning. We knew how the picture was going to end before we started. Everybody had written about the gunfight at O.K. Corral, but we wrote our own version of it. But that was why the picture was made. That was one thing that everybody, Western fan or not—and I was never an aficionado of the West, although I liked to see Western pictures—everybody had heard about the gunfight at O.K. Corral. But nobody really knew much about what it was.

Int.: So that it gave you a good deal of freedom.

Miller: Yes. We knew it was going to be the Earps against the Clantons.

Int.: In interviews Ford gave about his work, he mentions his unhappiness with the ending of *My Darling*

Clementine. He claims that he wanted Wyatt to stay in Tombstone and marry Clementine and that the studio forced another ending on him. Do you remember such a conflict?

Miller: First time I've heard that.

Int.: The ending as we see it is in the shooting script and, as you've told me, Ford was involved in its preparation.

Miller: He may have had second thoughts later, after I was long gone, but there was never any question of Earp's not going on to California.

Int.: How was *Clementine* received when it was released?

Miller: As I recall, the reviews were good. It wasn't treated as any classic or anything, because basically it was still just a Western although it happened to be done in Ford's style, which made it a step up. It was considered to be a good commercial picture, and reviewers who expected to see more depth in things from Ford probably were disappointed. But it was a commitment he had had with Fox left over from before the war.

Int.: But when you were working with him on *Clementine*, he didn't give you the impression that it was an assignment he didn't take much pleasure in, did he?

Miller: No, he liked it. He loved this kind of stuff. It was right up his alley. Everybody was very gung-ho for several reasons. As I say, it was the first picture for all of us after from three to five years' absence from the business. And Ford liked it; it was the kind of story he really liked, where he could be in on the creation and guide the creation of it with a cast he liked very much. No, everything was great until Zanuck made some changes behind him.

Int.: Some of that may have been re-editing scenes, as well as eliminating scenes from the film, then?

Miller: Oh, yes. I'm sure it was. I don't know chapter and verse because I never saw Ford's first cut, so I don't know what Zanuck did. I know Zanuck felt he could improve it. Ford liked a deliberate pace; Zanuck liked a fast pace. I think Ford felt that Zanuck possibly had destroyed the rhythm that he felt was so important, that was one of his trademarks. Zanuck was probably more impatient.

I liked to write lean and spare dialogue; that's what I always used to do and everybody that hired me knew it. But Ford, once on the set, would frequently cut things down even more. He felt anything he could get over without dialogue suited him fine. You can always do that once you've got actors there in front of you. Especially if it's Henry Fonda. But once Ford went with Argosy I guess nobody ever went behind him.

Int.: He did go back and do other studio projects after that, though.

Miller: As I remember it now, he stayed on long after his heyday. I didn't think his later pictures worked as well. I forget which pictures they were now. I just remember at the time thinking this is not vintage Ford. And the times changed too. He made a series of good Westerns after *My Darling Clementine*, but I didn't think his last few pictures were up to his high standards.

Reviews

The initial reviews of *My Darling Clementine*, while complimentary about Ford's direction and about the visual beauty of the film, tended to be patronizing about the subject matter, calling the film a "horse opera" or a "riproaring saga." Those critics, however, who did take the Western as a genre seriously were dismayed: Manny Farber found *Clementine* a "slowpoke cowboy epic" ruined by Ford's pictorializing, and Robert Warshow claimed that Ford's "unhappy preoccupation with style" reduced his material to a "sentimental legend of rural America." In the reviews reprinted here, Bosley Crowther's represents a common reaction in the popular press at the time, while Richard Griffith offers one of the more perceptive of the early responses to the film.

New York Times Review

Bosley Crowther

Let's be specific about this: The eminent director, John Ford, is a man who has a way with a Western like nobody in the picture trade. Seven years ago his classic *Stagecoach* snuggled very close to fine art in this genre. And now, by George, he's almost matched it with *My Darling Clementine*.

Not quite, it is true—for this picture, which came to the Rivoli yesterday, is a little too burdened with conventions of Western fiction to place it on a par. Too obvious a definition of heroes and villains is observed, and the standardized aspect of romance is too neatly and respectably entwined. But a dynamic composition of Western legend and scenery is still achieved. And the rich flavor of frontiering wafts in overpowering redolence from the screen.

In this particular instance, Mr. Ford and Twentieth Century-Fox are telling an oft-repeated story from the treasury of Western lore. It's the story of that famous frontier marshal who "cleaned up" Tombstone, Ariz.— Wyatt Earp. And if that doesn't place him precisely in the history catalogue,

From *New York Times*, December 4, 1946.

rest assured that he's been a model for film heroes ever since the days of William S. Hart. And since legend is being respected, as well as the conventions of the screen, it is the story of Wyatt's dauntless conquest of a gang of rustlers and a maiden's heart.

But even with standard Western fiction—and that's what the script has enjoined—Mr. Ford can evoke fine sensations and curiously captivating moods. From the moment that Wyatt and his brothers are discovered on the wide and dusty range, trailing a herd of cattle to a far-off promised land, a tone of pictorial authority is struck— and it is held. Every scene, every shot is the product of a keen and sensitive eye—an eye which has deep comprehension of the beauty of rugged people and a rugged world.

As the set for this film, a fine facsimile of frontier Tombstone was patiently built in the desert of Monument Valley, and it was there that Mr. Ford shot most of the picture. And he is a man who knows that Westerns belong, in the main, out of doors. When he catches a horseman or a stagecoach thumping across the scrubby wastes, the magnificence of nature—the sky and desert—dwarf the energies of man. Yet his scenes of intensity and violence are played very much to the fore, with the rawness and meanness of the frontier to set his vital human beings in relief.

New Movies Review

Richard Griffith

John Ford's new production comes as reassurance and uplift to all who believe in the future of the screen as an independent medium of expression communicating experience in a manner unique to its own special powers. On the surface, and to millions of its audiences, it will appear as no more than a jimdandy Western. It's all of that. It is also a sustained and complex work of the imagination.

Its thin and sometimes preposterous story is no more substantial than those which serve as groundwork for the big gaudy Westerns we have been getting lately, the *Abilene Towns*, *Renegades*, and *Canyon Passages*. An incident in the half-fictional lives of the Western gunmen Wyatt Earp and Doc Holliday, it centers throughout around familiar themes—the veteran frontier marshal drafted by the citizens of Tombstone to clean up the town, his friendly rivalry with the town's leading gambler and sharp-shooter, his long pursuit of the murderers of two of his brothers, and the final, climactic gun battle. What matters is not the plot, moving as it does from incident to incident without

From *New Movies* 22 (January 1947):6–8.

much consistency or connection, but the manner in which the director has derived from these materials the portrait of an era and the characters who peopled it.

The "legend" of the film director is frequently exposed in print these days. He is, we have been told a great many times, no longer the dictator of the silent days but merely an artisan whose secondary function it is to guide the stars through their paces while spelling out the script exactly as written and as handed to him by the omnipotent producer. That this is true as of this month and year, there can be no question. Whether it has come about as a by-product of an assembly-line system of production, or because there have arisen few talented directors in recent years, is food for speculation. But Mr. Ford reveals to us all over again that it need not be true, and that when a director fully commands his medium he can produce a work whose qualities owe little or nothing to writing, however fine, acting, however expert, production, however lavish. In *My Darling Clementine*, as in nearly all of the masterpieces of the movies, it is the director's hand and eye which furnish forth the scene. And again, as so often in the past, the artistic process which we see at work reminds us less of writing and acting and the other crafts of the theater than it does of music and poetry and dance, the arts which gain their effects through rhythmic movement. Every sequence in this film has its own decided tempo, each of which in measured progression contributes to the tempo of the whole. All other elements in the film are subordinated to that developing rhythm. The aptest analogy is that to music, where notes form chords, chords harmonies. As Iris Barry once said of *The Threepenny Opera*, "this film has been composed."

How is it done? In *My Darling Clementine* by a very interesting process indeed. The settings of the story are familiar to banality—the arid plains, the bare Western town, the bar-room, the cheap hotel. The ordinary Western uses them merely as backdrops against which physical action is played. Here they become the story itself. Consider this: the film opens as four cowboys drive a herd of cattle over the immense and desolate prairie; we look at the lowering skies, the charging steers, hear their bellowing and the cowboys' shouts. A wagon drives up, there is colloquy between its occupants and one of the cowboys, but we hardly listen to what is said, we are too immersed in scanning the weatherbeaten faces, looking beyond them to the cattle, the horses, the endless horizon. It is the scene and the action that dominate, that communicate, that give meaning to the slight

dialogue. Another time, in a saloon, when two gunmen take each other's measure at the bar, it is the silence, and the camera roving over the scared faces of the onlookers, the shining bar, the thrust-back chairs, that knot the tension and draw the spectator intimately into the scene. Silence and the roving camera, and the multiple positions of the camera, lend its intolerable excitement to the final gunfight when four men walk through town in the dawn toward their enemies ambushed at the end of the street. Many will exclaim over the beauty of the photography in this picture. Its technical excellence is less to the point than its functionalism. Again and again the camera seeks out those details of scene and action which not only clothe the story but actually tell it. It is out of their purposiveness that the illusion of beauty is created.

All this is far more than an exercise in film direction. Undoubtedly its qualities derive from Mr. Ford's affection for the portrait he is drawing—the portrait of the Old West. It is a mixed portrait, half-truth, half folklore, but fact or fancy, it is the West as Americans still feel it in their bones. There is that about the scene as Ford draws it that brings forth in the spectator some dim recognition as of memory or inheritance, remote, perhaps, from our twentieth-century scene, but whose kinship is not to be denied. It is in the very look of things, in the clothes the characters wear, the bone structure of their faces, the tempo of their speech. The director has been as successful with the people in the film as with their vast arena. Unlettered, inarticulate men, slow to speak because slow to decide (and how the tempo of the film measures that slowness of thinking and decision), quick to act because always in danger. And beyond this, with a sensitive, animal awareness of the beauty of their surroundings and of the extremes of evil and good in the humankind they encounter in a land where all are newcomers and strangers to each other.

Mr. Ford has again had the help of Henry Fonda. Of all our accomplished players, Mr. Fonda best understands and imagines the Western American, as he has proven three times over, in *The Grapes of Wrath*, *The Ox-Bow Incident*, and now in this. This can scarcely be accidental; Mr. Fonda is as surely the conscious interpreter of a vanished temperament as though he were a historian or psychologist. The dominant personage in the whole fascinating scene, he works on equal terms with the setter of the scene himself. The other players, excellent as they are, seem more nearly pliable instruments of the director, chosen for some physical trait or quirk of speech and outlook. Victor Mature is hardly

an obvious choice for the role of a tubercular gunman concealing under silken menace his despair at the loss of a Boston medical career, and his recital of a soliloquy from *Hamlet* does not suggest college speech. But the performance comes off amazingly. Mr. Mature's face is basilisk, his eyes look inward; in detail of manner and appearance he successfully suggests the desperate remittance-man. Other evocative roles are played by J. Farrell MacDonald—it's good to see his wise old face again—and Alan Mowbray, who makes the most of excellent opportunities as a rum-soaked ham, more familiar with *Ten Nights in a Barroom* than with *Hamlet*, but sporting the assurance of Booth or Irving. Tim Holt and Ward Bond are pleasingly right as brothers of Fonda.

The ladies fare not so well, because their roles are too much bound up with plot contrivances to seem real. Cathy Downs is the colorless Clementine of the title, who's come all the way from Boston to restore Mr. Mature to his rightful place among the elite of the Hub. Linda Darnell has an impossible assignment as Chihuahua, made up to look like a Hollywood version of a Mexican dance-hall girl. The necessity to build her role to stellar proportions tempts Mr. Ford to the film's one aberration, an operation scene which, though well done, is theatrical and meaningless.

But, as suggested earlier, it is the environment and the characters that grow out of it that mean more than plot or event. Behind the incidents which involve the principal players, one is conscious all the time of the surging life of the town, the church-building, cattle-growing, buying and selling, which was building a new land in this wild country. There is form and significance to this; it reaches out to us across the decades. Seeing it is often like being a boy in a small country town, ambling along the dusty street and watching the idlers with their feet up on the hotel porch railing of a slow Sunday morning.

Commentaries

Among later commentators on Ford and on the film, Lindsay Anderson is especially eloquent on Ford's stature as an artist. This British director has long admired Ford and has written frequently about his work; Anderson once said that he first understood film as an art form when, as a student at Oxford, he saw *My Darling Clementine*.

The three final selections in this section are appraisals of Ford's work by film scholars. Michael Budd's essay looks closely at some of the visual patterns in Ford's Westerns; Peter Wollen tracs thematic oppositions that constitute Ford's signature in three of his most celebrated films; Jim Kitses considers the Western as a genre, defining significant elements in a form that Ford explored with greater mastery than any other director.

John Ford

Lindsay Anderson

If it is ever permissible to divide an artist's life (which no doubt has seemed to him a constant and unbroken struggle) into neatly docketed periods, the years between 1939 and 1946 may be said to form a rich and generally cohesive one in Ford's career. From *Young Mr. Lincoln* his progress was rapid and triumphant. In the following seven years—three of which were taken up with service in the Navy—he made five further pictures whose poetry sprang up recognizably from the same source. Two of these were set similarly in the past: *Drums Along the Mohawk*, which immediately followed *Lincoln*, and *My Darling Clementine*, in 1946. The others were contemporary subjects: *The Grapes of Wrath* (1939), *Tobacco Road* (1940), and *They Were Expendable* (1945). (Possibly one would class also with these his documentary, *The Battle of Midway*, made in 1942— were one able now to see it.) On the face of it, few of these subjects have much relation to each other; in the hands of two different directors, it is difficult to imagine that the films of

From *Cinema* (*Beverly Hills*) 5–6 (Spring 1971):35–36.

The Grapes of Wrath and *My Darling Clementine* would have emerged with much in common. To Ford, however, all these stories proved to have elements stimulating to his particular kind of poetic imagination, and that imagination is everywhere visible in the films he made of them. In its own way, and with its own emphasis, each presents a variation on a constant theme.

This theme, first and last, is human. However full of incident their stories may be—and in all of them, with their battles and chases, their gunfights and slapstick humor, the element of action is pronounced—it is the people who remain the raison d'être of these films, and who give such happenings an excitement and meaning beyond their merely external impact. Ford's human allegiance is unqualified; the dignity and value per se of the human creature is a truth he holds to be self-evident, and his characters, presented with love and always an element of wonder, have a habit of suddenly taking on the stature of heroes. This is true not only in obvious instances like that of the dispossessed, indomitable wanderers of *The Grapes of Wrath*, or the sailors of *They Were Expendable*, who are left at the end of the campaign to meet death or captivity with spirit still unbroken. Time after time, he will halt the progress of a film to concentrate on a face or an attitude, not with the glancing stroke of one who makes an apt marginal observation, but with a deliberate enlargement of the detail until it seems to carry for that moment the whole weight and intention of the picture. In *They Were Expendable* the quite subordinate character of the old trader who has spent all of his life building up his post, and who refuses to desert it to the Japanese ("I've worked forty years for this, son; if I leave it, they'll have to carry me out"), is last seen in a wordless shot, sitting on the steps of his shack. He shifts his keg of whiskey to his side, lays his shotgun across his knees, and waits. And the film waits with him, till the scene dissolves to the river, with night falling, and the image fades. Without a word, and with a minimum of action, a comment has been made. The first sequence of *My Darling Clementine* ends with a held shot that similarly illuminates. The four Earp brothers, driving their cattle to California, have finished supper on the trail. Three of them mount and ride off to spend the evening in Tombstone, leaving their youngest brother to watch the herd. The boy watches them ride away, calling their names: "Goodnight, Wyatt —Goodnight Morg—Goodnight Virg . . ." They have disappeared, but still he stands there, and still the camera lingers on his face. Shots such as these are true film poetry, not pre-

planned in the script or on the drawing board, not juggled together in the cutting room, but created at that stage where the process must be at its most intense, when the director is most immediately and intimately in contact with his material—the camera, the actors, and the situation.

The skill with which these moments of significant pause are integrated into the narrative shows more than a masterly technical grasp; more fundamentally, it is the result of a sureness of aim, an uncompromising consistency of viewpoint that enables Ford, without betrayal or self-contradiction, to alternate mood and accent in the most daring fashion. In the long trial scene in *Young Mr. Lincoln*, the prosecuting counsel's cliché-packed, histrionic declamations are presented with the heightened emphasis of farce; yet the direct cuts to the two accused boys, or to the agonized face of their mother, or to Lincoln himself, stern and anxious for all his homespun humor, "come off" without a jar. An even more striking example is the whole of *Tobacco Road*, which for the extraordinary balance and control of its continual variations of mood—wistfully elegiac and wildly slapstick, cruelly satirical and tenderly sentimental—constitutes perhaps the most sheerly virtuoso performance of Ford's career.

Without a highly cultivated technique, effects of such subtlety would be impossible; but style is more than technique, and these films are poetic by virtue of their style. It is not that this ever obtrudes itself, breaking into or away from the narrative. Ford remains always a storyteller. In contrast with other poetic film makers—Dovzhenko, for instance, with whose vision his own has not a few qualities in common—he never goes outside the immediate dramatic context to find his symbols. It is rather a question of intensity within the flow of the drama. Constantly the images are charged with an emotional force so strong that, while continuing to perform a quite straightforward narrative function, they acquire as it were a second dimension of existence and meaning: what they are saying becomes inseparable from the way they are saying it. In the last reel of *Tobacco Road*, as Jeeter and Ada are being driven (as they think) to the poor farm, a succession of sustained close-ups on their tired, defeated faces, conveys not only this, but also, through this, the pathos of decrepit and abandoned old age, and, on a deeper level still, the eternal riddle of human dignity and transience. This powerful use of close-up, as affirmation or silently to reveal an inner state, is characteristic in Ford. Its stylistic complement are the long-shots which relate his men and women to the world about them. Two silhouet-

ted figures cross the dark crest of a hill against a cold early morning sky; a column of soldiers marches off into the distance; an old truck chugs persistently on, up the broad, far-stretching highway; a man on horseback rides away, and away . . . The films are full of far views and slow departures, gravely setting the gloried figure of man—"the brave, the mighty, and the wise"—in his mortal perspective.

Every poet is to some extent occupied in creating in his work his own, particular image of the world; and, for all his sense of the uniqueness of men, Ford's world is far from being bounded by the individual. His vision is rounded by its emphasis on the relations of men with one another and with the world in which they find themselves; on life lived in community; on all the hazards and rewards of physical existence. The scenes of action in these films thus become something more than mere occasions for excitement; they reflect a philosophy that finds virtue in activity, seeing struggle as a necessary element in life. Ford is never happier than when he is telling a story that illustrates these principles in their most direct and simple terms: all his excursions into America's past are fired by a kindling sympathy with the idea of life in a pioneering community, in the tough, disorderly mining township of Tombstone in *My Darling Clemen-*

tine, or amongst the hardy settlers of *Drums Along the Mohawk*, who have the natural perils of country and climate to contend with, as well as the savagery of Indian marauders and the British enemy. In such stories the disasters of war and the threats of lawlessness serve to throw into relief the necessary ideals of love and comradeship—which find their expression not only in acts of sacrifice and mutual aid, but in the scenes of celebration and conviviality, of dances, processions and games, which none of these films, with the exception of *Tobacco Road*, is without. (It is no coincidence that the sprightly jig to which young Mr. Lincoln clumsily steers Mary Todd round a Springfield ballroom is the very same as that to which Sheriff Earp takes the floor with Clementine Carter, to dance in the open air on a sunny Sunday morning, on the site of the first church in Tombstone.) Just as, on the individual plane, Ford's belief in the dignity of the simplest and humblest of his characters gives them from time to time a heroic enlargement, so, in the sphere of action, their deeds, conflicts and relationships acquire a corresponding poetic power of suggestion, bearing witness to the general theme—the theme of the good life. Hardihood and enterprise are qualities of this life, and also love.

The ideal of love which arouses the deepest response in Ford, and which has certainly inspired his most eloquent passages of poetry, is not that most habitual in the cinema: none of these films can adequately be described as a "love story." Even where there is a hero with a heroine to win or to lose, it is not the emotional progress of their relationship that gives the picture its heart. This is by no means to say that Ford's heroines are nothing more than obligatory ciphers. They are always individuals in their own right, people of spirit and resolution as well as charm: Lana Martin (in *Drums Along the Mohawk*) accepts with courage and good humor the hard lot of a pioneer's wife; Clementine is a determined girl, though quiet; and Sandy, the nurse in *They Were Expendable*, does her job with strictness as well as sweetness, with a moral devotion that is made to seem as important as love. Ford is not interested in stressing the specifically sexual elements in the relationships between his men and women; he is content to leave temperamental and sensual intimacies and conflicts largely unexplored. Instead the emphasis is on women as the helpmates of man, as wife and mother—the ministering angel rather than the coy and uncertain mistress. (Even Clementine has been trained as a nurse.) The great and most significant relationships are those of family and community, of comradeship, of the shared struggle for survival; the bitterest wrongs are those of social and economic injustice, of the persecution or exploitation of men by men. "I will plant companionship thick as trees along all the rivers of America . . ." The democratic vision of these films recalls that of an earlier, equally warm-blooded American poet—Walt Whitman.

One is unlikely to be able to assert such values without moments of anger. "What the Hell else does a man live for?" Ford had said in 1936 to an interviewer who had asked him whether he believed, as a director, in including in his pictures his point of view about "things that bothered him." And he quoted as an example an anti-lynching plea that he had put into *Judge Priest*, but which had been cut out of the finished film, for reasons of space. "It was one of the most scorching things you ever heard." He was to wait until 1952, when he inserted the same episode into *The Sun Shines Bright*, for an opportunity to get the sequence realized; but the same fierce sentiment is evident often elsewhere in his work: in the bitter trial scenes in *The Prisoner of Shark Island*; in the attempted lynching in *Young Mr. Lincoln*; and in the numerous incidents of exploitation and thuggery in *The Grapes of Wrath*. That the last impression of these pictures is never one of denial or defeat is not the result of compromise or false resolution. The wrongs are countered and the anger purged by the passionate affirmation of the opposite ideal, of human solidarity. Settlers and brothers; the family and the unit: the mother who refuses to betray one of her sons to justice to save the life of the other; the commander struggling to preserve the unity of his squadron; Ma Joad fighting to keep the family together—these are the persistent symbols. Disintegration is the tragedy; the derelict, hopeless community of share-croppers left withering on the burnt-out tobacco lands of the South; the farmer's family uprooted and splitting into fragments; the Motor Torpedo Boat squadron dwindling away man by man and boat by boat, until all that remains is a handful of men wandering down a deserted beach. Such stories would legitimately—one might think inevitably—end without hope; but for Ford acceptance of defeat seems not to be possible. Instead, each time, the music shifts into the major key, the beat is resumed, and the last images state positively: the living pathos of Jeeter Lester; the resurgence of hope in Ma Joad; and, over the heads of the men who were expendable, the plane soaring out, the struggle continued, the words "We Shall Return."

A Home in the Wilderness: Visual Imagery in John Ford's Westerns

Michael Budd

It has frequently been noted that the Western genre as a tradition in film and literature is based on a series of related oppositions—civilization and savagery, culture and nature, East and West, settlement and wilderness. These abstract themes and concepts are given definite form in individual films. Every director who has constructed a distinctive Western world in his films has made images with which to visualize and particularize the meanings latent in these abstract elements. In many of the films of Budd Boetticher, for example, towns and settlements are virtually absent, fertile oases in the desert providing the only resting places for travelers. In the Westerns of Sam Peckinpah the walled-in squares of Mexican villages are transformed from places of peace and refuge into traps, locations for the most extreme outbursts of violence. And Sergio Leone makes his sleepy little towns into labyrinths,

From Michael Budd, "A Home in the Wilderness: Visual Imagery in John Ford's Westerns," *Cinema Journal* 16 (Fall 1976):62–75.

every door and window potentially hiding a gunman. The cinematic world of each of these directors is delineated by recurrent images, images which make visual a particular version of the general Western oppositions, which select from and inflect the range of possibilities present in the genre.

In the Westerns of John Ford, civilization is embodied primarily in the family and the community, and characteristically located in homes, cavalry forts, stagecoaches, covered wagons, or other shelters. This study examines a visual tradition in which home and shelter is juxtaposed with its opposite, the desert wilderness, within single images. The tradition is a recurrent complex of images which, in various ways, relates home space to wilderness space, bringing them into visual confrontation within the frame. The encounter of home and wilderness is more than a theme in Ford's Westerns: it is a central, formative viewpoint, a way of looking at the world.

The viewpoint is communicated visually by a *frame* within the larger frame. Shots looking through doors, through windows, gates, porches, and canopies bring indoors and outdoors into juxtaposition. Such images are sufficiently pervasive to suggest a structuring vision of the nature of the frontier itself. Images using a frame are a central aspect of the visual organization which complements the narrative in every film. Despite differences in many elements, the visual encounter of inside and outside, home and desert, refuge and danger appears throughout, and helps to define each film as a part of the whole group. Virtually every film has its distinctive variation of the frame-within-a-frame configuration, but every film also contains variations found in other films. The complex of home-wilderness images seems central to the similarities among Ford's Westerns: not only does it bring together the underlying elements of the genre, connecting the dynamics of the Western to the specific concerns of the director, but it also permeates the formal pattern and texture of the films. The meeting of home and wilderness, the edge of the frontier, is constituted in the design of the images themselves.

In *My Darling Clementine* the wilderness is a more benign presence. Though it harbors the murderous Clantons, its openness and freedom are more emphasized; the bright sky dominates. Thus the relation between two kinds of space connoted by the frame image is a kind of balance, a counterpoising, rather than a threat or invasion by the wilderness as in *Stagecoach*. The earlier film takes a vulnerable society out of the safety of its towns and exposes it to the transforming effects of the frontier through the gradual dissolution of its protective frames, its fences, walls, and gates. *My Darling Clementine* places the town of Tombstone at the moment of taming, with the newborn community in visual equilibrium with its ancient surroundings.

Thus the film's distinctive variation on the frame image is its extensive exploration of the long porch, the meeting point between shelter and wilderness. The town's single street has buildings on only one side, and so is open to the desert. The porch extends the shelter of the buildings, yet is penetrated by the outdoors and the slanting sunlight, which so often brings the outdoors inside in these films. Under the porch, at the juncture of sunlight and shadow, Wyatt takes his place as protector. The combination of spaces is continually framed from just under or outside the porch roof: the edge of the frontier is not a hard line drawn by civilization as in *Stagecoach*, but a beneficent interpenetration of the expansive wilderness with the refuge of human cover, which results in the birth of a new community.

Placed between enclosure and vast space, porches are a characteristic location for mediating heroes, whether defenders like Wyatt Earp or outsiders like Ethan Edwards in *The Searchers*. Rocking chairs, reminders of rest in old age, appear frequently on porches, and the churchgoers in *My Darling Clementine* are briefly seen rocking on the hotel porch after Sunday dinner. Just as old people sit on a porch to look outward from home, young lovers find it a place to be alone together, to escape temporarily the community's presence. Michael and Philadelphia in *Fort Apache*, Brad and Lucy in *The Searchers*, Tom and Mary in *Sergeant Rutledge*, Jim and Marty in *Two Rode Together*—for all these pairs the porch is an appropriate setting for courtship. And where there is no sheltering porch, a couple moves naturally to the edge of settlement for privacy, as do Dallas and Ringo in *Stagecoach*, and Olivia and Flint in *She Wore a Yellow Ribbon*. In both these cases the periphery is at once a place of danger and of new closeness between man and woman.

In *My Darling Clementine*, the imagery of porches and of Tombstone's boundaries culminates in the famous Sunday morning sequence when Clementine joins Wyatt for the church dance. The sequence brings together the many connotations of intermingled home and wilderness space in the film. It begins by evoking the porch as a *place* as never before. The narrative slows almost to a halt; as Wyatt walks casually out of the barbershop and down the long porch to take his accustomed spot, the flow of pioneers and their wagons past him toward the church is a continuous presence in image and sound; immersion in setting replaces action. Actually, a new momentum, a sea change is beginning: the events surrounding Wyatt, Doc, and Clementine are poised for resolution, and the movement of the churchgoers provides the impetus. Barbershop, hotel lobby, porch, street, and desert—the acute sense of the continuity of these spaces seems in itself to draw Clementine and Wyatt from one to the other, on and on. Countering the associations of the desert with the murderous Clantons, the pioneers converge on the town from outside, pass through its center and on to the half-built church on the outskirts. They seem to bear the townspeople with them, as if to join the two areas at a meeting point.

Clementine and Wyatt complete this movement in their walk from the town's center to its edge, extending the frontier by establishing a new center. They leave the shelter of frames and porches for a church without walls. Appropriately, the dance is being held to raise money to put up a roof: it is the precise moment when wilderness becomes home. The two kinds of space seem to merge, as the pioneers celebrate the integration of natural and human order. The frame of the church steeple is open to the sky; virtually every shot places the dancers against horizon and sky; the sequence builds and builds.

The church dance sequence forms a crescendo to the measured tempo of Sunday morning in Tombstone and is divided into five smaller sequences, each part a minor crescendo carrying toward the larger climax. The various elements of the scene—the couple, the town, the church and its people, the surrounding buttes—are analyzed and synthesized in a new unification of spaces and forces.

In the first part, Wyatt and Clementine move away from Tombstone's enclosures, and the camera marks a growing sense of spaciousness. The church is shown only in extreme long shot, and the congregation is an undifferentiated mass, the ringing bell and the hymn heard from afar. The couple is separated spatially from their destination, and they recede at the end of this first part toward the faraway gathering at the edge of town.

The second part explores the church scene itself, isolating its elements and bringing us closer into its spirit. Elder Simpson celebrates the transition from hymn to dance music, the musicians are seen in individual medium shots, and the dancers whirl between rows of clapping participants. And closer long shots of the entire church make the mass now a group of individual people. The music comes up as the dancers become ani-mated; we watch the community being created.

The third part of the sequence intercuts Wyatt and Clementine, standing to the side, with the increasing ebullient dancers. Couple and community are in separate shots; the dance continues to build, while Wyatt and Clementine, not yet participants, are more and more attracted to it. The parallel actions culminate in the final three shots of this part. The dancers begin a movement of both lines through the center, a climactic affirmation of communal unity. Only then, in the next shot, are the town and the far-off monuments added to the church scene, all elements in the film accumulating in one synoptic image in preparation for the couple's inclusion. And so when Wyatt subsequently asks Clementine to dance, and they start to join the community, the action carries a tremendous charge of assimilation and consummation. Separate spaces, sounds, and forces are joined; the community finds a center; from bell to hymn to dance, the rising music draws everything together.

In the fourth part, Wyatt and Clementine join the celebration, and the parallel lines of dancers in previous shots become a circle around them as they dance, a circle of people who are the church's only walls. The marshal and his lady fair dance in their

"Promised Land" as the Mormons in *Wagon Master* do not, because their arrival at the church celebrates a journey like the Mormons', a civilizing act. The church is not a destination but a process.

Finally, in the fifth and final part of the sequence, Morgan and Virgil drive up in the wagon to watch, surprised, as Wyatt dances enthusiastically with Clementine. Now the pattern of part three is varied: Wyatt has acquired a new family and community, his older loyalties left behind (temporarily), his brothers separated spatially as he was earlier. And in accordance with the progression throughout the entire sequence, the shots get closer and closer. The camera tilts up as the couple dances toward it, and records their smiling faces as they whirl by. The five-part sequence moves from the porch shelters of Tombstone to the open air of the church, accumulating the town and surrounding desert, and placing the civilizing couple at the community's center. In this prolonged moment of frontier, the landscape is ambiguously harsh and beautiful, and pioneers need no shelter: at the leading edge of civilization, home and wilderness are united.

At the end of the film, Wyatt's approach to the gunfire at the O.K. Corral is structured like the couple's earlier approach to the church dance.

Why? The Clantons bring their violence through town and go out again to its edges, just as the pioneers earlier brought a pacific community through town and out to its edges. The pioneer's movement to the church unified Tombstone and made it more secure; Wyatt's second walk to the town's frontier defends the meaning of the first. So Wyatt stands under a roof and Old Man Clanton outside it as Wyatt curses him away after the gunfight: the marshal makes a shelter of the corral just as he and Clementine completed the open church.

At the end, Wyatt and Morgan ride away in a shot almost identical to the one at the beginning of *Stagecoach* in which the coach and cavalry escort begin the journey. Again the travelers pass the wooden fence signifying the edge of civilization; the road leads straight toward the same spire-like monument on the horizon. In *Stagecoach*, the open fence comes to suggest the pioneers' flimsy defenses. In *My Darling Clementine* the same fence is like the frame of the church steeple, connoting the freedom at the juncture of home and wilderness. Wyatt may begin a new *Stagecoach* adventure at the end of *My Darling Clementine*, but whereas the earlier film is one of barriers broken and reinforced, Wyatt's world is morally and spatially continuous.

Structural Patterns in John Ford's Films

Peter Wollen

. . . Geoffrey Nowell-Smith has summed up the *auteur* theory as it is normally presented today:

> One essential corollary of the theory as it has been developed is the discovery that the defining characteristics of an author's work are not necessarily those which are most readily apparent. The purpose of criticism thus becomes to uncover behind the superficial contrasts of subject and treatment a hard core of basic and often recondite motifs. The pattern formed by these motifs . . . is what gives an author's work its particular structure, both defining it internally and distinguishing one body of work from another.

It is this "structural approach," as Nowell-Smith calls it, which is indispensable for the critic.

The test case for the *auteur* theory is provided by the work of Howard Hawks. Why Hawks, rather than, say, Frank Borzage or King Vidor? First,

From Peter Wollen, "The Auteur Theory," in *Signs and Meanings in the Cinema* (Bloomington: Indiana University Press, 1972) 80–82, 93–101.

Hawks is a director who has worked for years within the Hollywood system. His first film, *Road to Glory*, was made in 1926. Yet throughout his long career he has only once received general critical acclaim, for his wartime film, *Sergeant York*, which closer inspection reveals to be eccentric and atypical of the main *corpus* of Hawks's films. Second, Hawks has worked in almost every genre. He has made Westerns (*Rio Bravo*), gangster films (*Scarface*), war films (*Air Force*), thrillers (*The Big Sleep*), science fiction (*The Thing from Another World*), musicals (*Gentlemen Prefer Blondes*), comedies (*Bringing Up Baby*), even a biblical epic (*Land of the Pharaohs*). Yet all of these films (except perhaps *Land of the Pharaohs*, which he himself was not happy about) exhibit the same thematic preoccupations, the same recurring motifs and incidents, the same visual style and tempo. In the same way that Roland Barthes constructed a species of *homo racinianus*, the critic can construct a *homo hawksianus*, the protagonist of Hawksian values in the problematic Hawksian world.

Hawks achieved this by reducing the genres to two basic types: the adventure drama and the crazy comedy. These two types express inverse views of the world, the positive and negative poles of the Hawksian vision. Hawks stands opposed, on the one hand, to John Ford and, on the other hand, to Budd Boetticher. All these directors are concerned with the problem of heroism. For the hero, as an individual, death is an absolute limit which cannot be transcended: it renders the life which preceded it meaningless, absurd. How then can there be any meaningful individual action during life? How can individual action have any value—be heroic—if it cannot have transcendent value, because of the absolutely devaluing limit of death? John Ford finds the answer to this question by placing and situating the individual within society and within history, specifically within American history. Ford finds transcendent values in the historic vocation of America as a nation, to bring civilization to a savage land, the garden to the wilderness. At the same time, Ford also sees these values themselves as problematic; he begins to question the movement of American history itself. Boetticher, on the contrary, insists on a radical individualism. "I am not interested in making films about mass feelings. I am for the individual." He looks for values in the encounter with death itself: the underlying metaphor is always that of the bull-fighter in the arena. The hero enters a group of companions, but there is no possibility of group solidarity. Boetticher's hero acts by dissolving groups and collectivities of

any kind into their constituent individuals, so that he confronts each person face-to-face; the films develop, in Andrew Sarris's words, into "floating poker games, where every character takes turns at bluffing about his hand until the final showdown." Hawks, unlike Boetticher, seeks transcendent values beyond the individual, in solidarity with others. But, unlike Ford, he does not give his heroes any historical dimension, any destiny in time. . . .

In the films of Howark Hawks a systematic series of oppositions can be seen very near the surface, in the contrast between the adventure dramas and the crazy comedies. If we take the adventure dramas alone it would seem that Hawks's work is flaccid, lacking in dynamism; it is only when we consider the crazy comedies that it becomes rich, begins to ferment: alongside every dramatic hero we are aware of a phantom, stripped of mastery, humiliated, inverted. With other directors, the system of oppositions is much more complex: instead of there being two broad strata of films there is a whole series of shifting variations. In these cases, we need to analyze the roles of the protagonists themselves, rather than simply the worlds in which they operate. The protagonists of fairy-tales or myths, as Lévi-Strauss has pointed out, can be dissolved into bundles of differential elements, pairs of opposites. Thus the difference between the prince and the goose-girl can be reduced to two antinomic pairs: one natural, male versus female, and the other cultural, high versus low. We can proceed with the same kind of operation in the study of films, though, as we shall see, we shall find them more complex than fairy-tales.

It is instructive, for example, to consider three films of John Ford and compare their heroes: Wyatt Earp in *My Darling Clementine*, Ethan Edwards in *The Searchers* and Tom Doniphon in *The Man Who Shot Liberty Valance*. They all act within the recognizable Ford world, governed by a set of oppositions, but their *loci* within that world are very different. The relevant pairs of opposites overlap; different pairs are foregrounded in different movies. The most relevant are garden versus wilderness, ploughshare versus sabre, settler versus nomad, European versus Indian, civilized versus savage, book versus gun, married versus unmarried, East versus West. These antinomies can often be broken down further. The East, for instance, can be defined either as Boston or Washington and, in *The Last Hurrah*, Boston itself is broken down into the antipodes of Irish immigrants versus Plymouth Club, themselves bundles of such differ-

ential elements as Celtic versus Anglo-Saxon, poor versus rich, Catholic versus Protestant, Democrat versus Republican, and so on. At first sight, it might seem that the oppositions listed above overlap to the extent that they become practically synonymous, but this is by no means the case. As we shall see, part of the development of Ford's career has been the shift from an identity between civilized versus savage and European versus Indian to their separation and final reversal, so that in *Cheyenne Autumn* it is the Europeans who are savage, the victims who are heroes.

The master antinomy in Ford's films is that between the wilderness and the garden. As Henry Nash Smith has demonstrated, in his magisterial book *Virgin Land*, the contrast between the image of America as a desert and as a garden is one which has dominated American thought and literature, recurring in countless novels, tracts, political speeches and magazine stories. In Ford's films it is crystallized in a number of striking images. *The Man Who Shot Liberty Valance*, for instance, contains the image of the cactus rose, which encapsulates the antinomy between desert and garden which pervades the whole film. Compare with this the famous scene in *My Darling Clementine*, after Wyatt Earp has gone to the barber (who civilizes the unkempt), where the scent of honeysuckle is twice remarked upon: an artificial perfume, cultural rather than natural. This moment marks the turning-point in Wyatt Earp's transition from wandering cowboy, nomadic, savage, bent on personal revenge, unmarried, to married man, settled, civilized, the sheriff who administers the law.

Earp, in *My Darling Clementine*, is structurally the most simple of the three protagonists I have mentioned: his progress is an uncomplicated passage from nature to culture, from the wilderness left in the past to the garden anticipated in the future. Ethan Edwards, in *The Searchers*, is more complex. He must be defined not in terms of past versus future or wilderness versus garden compounded in himself, but in relation to two other protagonists: Scar, the Indian chief, and the family of homesteaders. Ethan Edwards, unlike Earp, remains a nomad throughout the film. At the start, he rides in from the desert to enter the log-house; at the end, with perfect symmetry, he leaves the house again to return to the desert, to vagrancy. In many respects, he is similar to Scar; he is a wanderer, a savage, outside the law: he scalps his enemy. But, like the homesteaders, of course, he is a European, the mortal foe of the Indian. Thus Edwards is ambiguous; the antinomies invade the personality of the protagonist himself.

The oppositions tear Edwards in two; he is a tragic hero. His companion, Martin Pawley, however, is able to resolve the duality; for him, the period of nomadism is only an episode, which has meaning as the restitution of the family, a necessary link between his old home and his new home.

Ethan Edwards's wandering is, like that of many other Ford protagonists, a quest, a search. A number of Ford films are built round the theme of the quest for the Promised Land, an American re-enactment of the biblical exodus, the journey through the desert to the land of milk and honey, the New Jerusalem. This theme is built on the combination of the two pairs: wilderness versus garden and nomad versus settler; the first pair precedes the second in time. Thus, in *Wagonmaster*, the Mormons cross the desert in search of their future home; in *How Green Was My Valley* and *The Informer*, the protagonists want to cross the Atlantic to a future home in the United States. But, during Ford's career, the situation of home is reversed in time. In *Cheyenne Autumn* the Indians journey in search of the home they once had in the past; in *The Quiet Man*, the American Sean Thornton returns to his ancestral home in Ireland. Ethan Edwards's journey is a kind of parody of this theme: his object is not constructive, to found a home, but destructive, to find and scalp Scar. Nevertheless, the weight of the film remains oriented to the future: Scar has burned down the home of the settlers, but it is replaced and we are confident that the homesteader's wife, Mrs. Jorgensen, is right when she says: "Some day this country's going to be a fine place to live." The wilderness will, in the end, be turned into a garden.

The Man Who Shot Liberty Valance has many similarities with *The Searchers*. We may note three: the wilderness becomes a garden—this is made quite explicit, for Senator Stoddart has wrung from Washington the funds necessary to build a dam which will irrigate the desert and bring real roses, not cactus roses; Tom Doniphon shoots Liberty Valance as Ethan Edwards scalped Scar; a log-home is burned to the ground. But the differences are equally clear: the log-home is burned after the death of Liberty Valance; it is destroyed by Doniphon himself; it is his own home. The burning marks the realization that he will never enter the Promised Land, that to him it means nothing; that he has doomed himself to be a creature of the past, insignificant in the world of the future. By shooting Liberty Valance he has destroyed the only world in which he himself can exist, the world of the gun rather than the book; it is as though Ethan Edwards had perceived that by scalping

Scar, he was in reality committing suicide. It might be mentioned too that, in *The Man Who Shot Liberty Valance*, the woman who loves Doniphon marries Senator Stoddart. Doniphon when he destroys his loghouse (his last words before doing so are "Home, sweet home!") also destroys the possibility of marriage.

The themes of *The Man Who Shot Liberty Valance* can be expressed in another way. Ransom Stoddart represents rational-legal authority, Tom Doniphon represents charismatic authority. Doniphon abandons his charisma and cedes it, under what amount to false pretenses, to Stoddart. In this way charismatic and rational-legal authority are combined in the person of Stoddart and stability thus assured. In *The Searchers* this transfer does not take place; the two kinds of authority remain separated. In *My Darling Clementine* they are combined naturally in Wyatt Earp, without any transfer being necessary. In many of Ford's late films—*The Quiet Man*, *Cheyenne Autumn*, *Donovan's Reef*— the accent is placed on traditional authority. The island of Ailakaowa, in *Donovan's Reef*, a kind of Valhalla for the homeless heroes of *The Man Who Shot Liberty Valance*, is actually a monarchy, though complete with the Boston girl, wooden church and saloon, made familiar by *My Darling Clementine*. In fact, the character of

Chihuahua, Doc Holliday's girl in *My Darling Clementine*, is split into two: Miss Lafleur and Lelani, the native princess. One represents the saloon entertainer, the other the non-American in opposition to the respectable Bostonians, Amelia Sarah Dedham and Clementine Carter. In a broad sense, this is a part of a general movement which can be detected in Ford's work to equate the Irish, Indians and Polynesians as traditional communities, set in the past, counterposed to the march forward to the American future, as it has turned out in reality, but assimilating the values of the American future as it was once dreamed.

Authorship and Genre: Notes on the Western

Jim Kitses

First of all, the Western is American history. Needless to say, this does not mean that the films are historically accurate or that they cannot be made by Italians. More simply, the statement means that American frontier life provides the milieu and *mores* of the Western, its wild bunch of cowboys, its straggling towns and mountain scenery. Of course westward expansion was to continue for over a century, the frontier throughout that period a constantly shifting belt of settlement. However, Hollywood's West has typically been, from about 1865 to 1890 or so, a brief final instant in the process. This twilight era was a momentous one: within just its span we can count a number of frontiers in the sudden rash of mining camps, the building of the railways, the Indian Wars, the cattle drives, the coming of the farmer. Together with the last days of the Civil War and the exploits of the badmen, here is the raw material of the Western.

At the heart of this material, and crucial to an understanding of the

From Jim Kitses, *Horizons West* (Bloomington: Indiana University Press, 1970) 8–26.

gifts the form holds out to its practitioners, is an ambiguous, mercurial concept: the idea of the West. From time immemorial the West has beckoned to statesmen and poets, existing as both a direction and a place, an imperialist theme and a pastoral Utopia. Great empires developed ever westward: from Greece to Rome, from Rome to Britain, from Britain to America. It was in the West as well that the fabled lands lay, the Elysian fields, Atlantis, El Dorado. As every American schoolboy knows, it was in sailing on his passage to India, moving ever westward to realize the riches of the East, that Columbus chanced on the New World. Hand in hand with the hope of fragrant spices and marvellous tapestries went the everbeckoning dream of life eternal: surely somewhere, there where the sun slept, was the fountain of youth.

As America began to be settled and moved into its expansionist phases, this apocalyptic and materialist vision found new expression. In his seminal study *Virgin Land*, Henry Nash Smith has traced how the West as symbol has functioned in America's history and consciousness. Is the West a Garden of natural dignity and innocence offering refuge from the decadence of civilization? Or is it a treacherous Desert stubbornly resisting the gradual sweep of agrarian progress and community values? Dominating

America's intellectual life in the nineteenth century, these warring ideas were most clearly at work in attitudes surrounding figures like Daniel Boone, Kit Carson and Buffalo Bill Cody, who were variously seen as rough innocents ever in flight from society's artifice, and as enlightened pathfinders for the new nation. A folk hero manufactured in his own time, Cody himself succumbed toward the end of his life to the play of these concepts that so gripped the imagination of his countrymen: "I stood between savagery and civilization most all my early days."

Refracted through and pervading the genre, this ideological tension has meant that a wide range of variation is possible in the basic elements of the form. The plains and mountains of Western landscape can be an inspiring and civilizing environment, a moral universe productive of the Western hero, a man with a code. But this view, popularized by Robert Warshow in his famous essay, "The Westerner," is one-sided. Equally the terrain can be barren and savage, surroundings so demanding that men are rendered morally ambiguous, or wholly brutalized. In the same way, the community in the Western can be seen as a positive force, a movement of refinement, order and local democracy into the wilds, or as a harbinger of corruption in the form of eastern

values which threaten frontier ways. This analysis oversimplifies in isolating the attitudes: a conceptually complex structure that draws on both images is the typical one. If eastern figures such as bankers, lawyers and journalists are often either drunkards or corrupt, their female counterparts generally carry virtues and graces which the West clearly lacks. And if Nature's harmonies produce the upright hero, they also harbor the animalistic Indian. Thus central to the form we have a philosophical dialectic, an ambiguous cluster of meanings and attitudes that provide the traditional thematic structure of the genre. This shifting ideological play can be described through a series of antinomies, so:

THE WILDERNESS	CIVILIZATION
The Individual	The Community
freedom	restriction
honor	institutions
self-knowledge	illusion
integrity	compromise
self-interest	social responsibility
solipsism	democracy
Nature	Culture
purity	corruption
experience	knowledge
empiricism	legalism
pragmatism	idealism

THE WILDERNESS	CIVILIZATION
brutalization	refinement
savagery	humanity
The West	The East
America	Europe
the frontier	America
equality	class
agrarianism	industrialism
tradition	change
the past	the future

In scanning this grid, if we compare the tops and tails of each subsection, we can see the ambivalence at work at its outer limits: the West, for example, rapidly moves from being the spearhead of manifest destiny to the retreat of ritual. What we are dealing with here, of course, is no less than a national world-view: underlying the whole complex is the grave problem of identity that has special meaning for Americans. The isolation of a vast unexplored continent, the slow growth of social forms, the impact of an unremitting New England Puritanism obsessed with the cosmic struggle of good and evil, of the elect and the damned, the clash of allegiances to Mother Country and New World, these factors are the crucible in which American consciousness was formed. The thrust of contradictions, everywhere apparent in American life and culture, is clearest in the great literary heritage of the romantic novel that springs from Fenimore Cooper and moves through Hawthorne and Melville, Mark Twain and Henry James, Fitzgerald and Faulkner, Hemingway and Mailer. As Richard Chase has underlined in his *The American Novel and Its Tradition*, this form in American hands has always tended to explore rather than to order, to reflect on rather than to moralize about, the irreconcilables that it confronts; and where contradictions are resolved the mode is often that of melodrama or the pastoral. For failing to find a moral tone and a style of close social observation—in short, for failing to be *English*—the American novel has often had its knuckles rapped. As with literature, so with the film: the prejudice that even now persists in many quarters of criticism and education with reference to the Hollywood cinema (paramountly in America itself) flows from a similar lack of understanding.

The ideology that I have been discussing inevitably filters through many of Hollywood's genres: the Western has no monopoly here. But what gives the form a particular thrust and centrality is its historical setting; its being placed at exactly that moment when options are still open, the dream of a primitivistic individualism, the ambivalence of at once beneficent and threatening horizons, still tenable. For the film-maker who is preoccupied with these motifs, the Western has offered a remarkably expressive canvas. Nowhere, of course, is the freedom that it bestows for personal expression more evident than in the cinema of John Ford.

It would be presumptuous to do more than refer here to this distinguished body of work, the crucial silent period of which remains almost wholly inaccessible. Yet Ford's career, a full-scale scrutiny of which must be a priority, stands as unassailable proof of how the historical dimensions of the form can be orchestrated to produce the most personal kind of art. As Andrew Sarris has pointed out, "no American director has ranged so far across the landscape of the American past." But the journey has been a long and deeply private one through green valleys of hope on to bitter sands of despair. The peak comes in the forties where Ford's works are bright monuments to his vision of the trek of the faithful to the Promised Land, the populist hope of an ideal community, a dream affectionately etched in *The Grapes of Wrath, My Darling Clementine, Wagonmaster*. But as the years slip by the darker side of Ford's romanticism comes to the foreground, and twenty years after the war—in *The Man who Shot Liberty Valance, Two Rode Together, Cheyenne Autumn*—we find a regret for the past, a bitterness at the larger role of Washington, and a desolation over the neglect of older values. The trooping of the colors has a different meaning now. As Peter Wollen has described in his chapter on *auteur* theory in *Signs and Meaning in the Cinema* [reprinted in this volume], the progression can be traced in the transposition of civilized and savage elements. The Indians of *Drums Along the Mohawk* and *Stagecoach*, devilish marauders that threaten the hardy pioneers, suffer a sea-change as Ford's hopes wane, until with *Cheyenne Autumn* they are a civilized, tragic people at the mercy of a savage community. The ringing of the changes is discernible in the choice of star as well, the movement from the quiet idealism of the early Fonda through the rough pragmatism of the Wayne *persona* to the cynical self-interest of James Stewart. As Ford grows older the American dream sours, and we are left with nostalgia for the Desert.

Imperious as he is, Ford is not the Western; nor is the Western history. For if we stand back from the Western, we are less aware of historical (or representational) elements than of form and *archetype*. This may sound platitudinous: for years critics have spoken confidently of the balletic movement of the genre, of pattern and variation, of myth. This last, ever in the air when the form is discussed, clouds the issues completely. We can speak of the genre's celebration of America, of the contrasting images of Garden and Desert, as national myth. We can speak of the parade of mythology that is mass culture, of which the Western is clearly a part. We can invoke Greek and medieval myth, referring to the Western hero as a latter-day knight, a contemporary Achilles. Or we can simply speak of the myth of the Western, a journalistic usage which evidently implies that life is not like that. However, in strict classical terms of definition, myth has to do with the activity of gods, and as such the Western has no myth. Rather, it incorporates elements of *displaced* (or corrupted) myth on a scale that can render them considerably more prominent than in most art. It is not surprising that little advance is made upon the clichés, no analysis undertaken that interprets how these elements are at work within a particular film or director's career. What are the archetypal elements we sense within the genre and how do they function? As Northrop Frye has shown in his monumental *The Anatomy of Criticism*, for centuries this immensely tangled ground has remained almost wholly unexplored in literature itself. The primitive state of film criticism inevitably reveals a yawning abyss in this direction.

Certain facts are clear. Ultimately the Western derives from the long and fertile tradition of Wild West literature that had dominated the mass taste of nineteenth-century America. Fenimore Cooper is again the germinal figure here: Nash Smith has traced how the roots of the formula, the adventures of an isolated, aged trapper/hunter (reminiscent of Daniel Boone) who rescues genteel heroines from the Indians, were in the *Leatherstocking Tales* which began to emerge in the 1820s. These works, fundamentally in the tradition of the sentimental novel, soon gave way to a rush of pulp literature in succeeding decades culminating in the famous series edited by Erastus Beadle which had astonishing sales for its time. Specialists in the adventure tale, the romance, the sea story, turned to the West for their setting to cash in on the huge market. As the appetite for violence and spectacle grew, variations followed, the younger hunter that had succeeded Cooper's hero losing his pristine nature and giving way to a morally ambiguous figure with a dark past, a Deadwood Dick who is finally redeemed by a woman's love. The genre, much of it subliterary, became increasingly hungry for innovation as the century wore on, its Amazon heroines perhaps only the most spectacular sign of a desperation at its declining hold on the imagination. As the actual drama of the frontier finally came to a close, marked by Frederick C. Turner's historic address before the American Historical Association in 1893 where he advanced his thesis on free land and its continual recession westward as the key factor in America's development, the vogue for the dime novel waned, its hero now frozen in the figure of the American cowboy.

In 1900 the Wild Bunch held up and robbed a Union Pacific railway train in Wyoming; in 1903 Edwin S. Porter made *The Great Train Robbery* in New Jersey. The chronology of these events, often commented on, seems less important than their geography: it had been the East as well from which Beadle Westerns such as *Seth Jones; or, The Captives of the Frontier* had flowed. The cinema was born, its novel visual apparatus at the ready, the heir to a venerable tradition of reworking history (the immediate past) in tune with ancient classical rhythms. In general, of course, the early silent cinema everywhere drew on and experimented with traditional and folkloric patterns for the forms it required. What seems remarkable about the Western, however, is that the core of a formulaic lineage already existed. The heart of this legacy was romantic narrative, tales which insisted on the idealization of characters who wielded near-magical powers. Recurrent confrontations between the personified forces of good and evil, testimony to the grip of the New

England Calvinist ethic, had soon focused the tales in the direction of morality play. However, in any case, the structure was an impure one which had interpolated melodramatic patterns of corruption and redemption, the revenge motif borrowed from the stage toward the end of the century, and humor in the Davy Crockett and Eastern cracker-barrel traditions. The physical action and spectacle of the Wild West shows, an offshoot of the penny-dreadful vogue, was to be another factor.

This complex inheritance meant that from the outset the Western could be many things. In their anecdotal *The Western*, George N. Fenin and William K. Everson have chronicled the proliferating, overlapping growth of early days: Bronco Billy Anderson's robust action melodramas, Thomas H. Ince's darker tales, W. S. Hart's more "authentic" romances, the antics of the virtuous Tom Mix, the Cruze and Ford epics of the twenties, the stunts and flamboyance of Ken Maynard and Hoot Gibson, the flood of "B" movies, revenge sagas, serials, and so on. Experiment seems always to have been varied and development dynamic, the pendulum swinging back and forth between opposing poles of emphasis on drama and history, plots and spectacle, romance and "realism," seriousness and comedy. At any point where audience response was felt the action could freeze, the industrial machine moving into high gear to produce a cycle and, in effect, establish a minor tradition within the form. Whatever "worked" was produced, the singing westerns of the thirties perhaps only the most prominent example of this policy of eclectic enterprise.

For many students of the Western, Gene Autry and Roy Rogers have seemed an embarrassing aberration. However, such a view presupposes that there is such an animal as *the* Western, a precise model rather than a loose, shifting and variegated genre with many roots and branches. The word "genre" itself, although a helpful one, is a mixed blessing: for many the term carries literary overtones of technical *rules*. Nor is "form" any better; the Western is many *forms*. Only a pluralist vision makes sense of our experience of the genre and begins to explain its amazing vigor and adaptability, the way it moves closer and further from our own world, brightening or darkening with each succeeding decade. Yet over the years critics have ever tried to freeze the genre once and for all in a definitive model of the "classical" Western. Certainly it must be admitted that works such as *Shane* and *My Darling Clementine* weld together in remarkable balance historical reconstruction

and national themes with personal drama and archetypal elements. In his essay, "The Evolution of the Western" Bazin declared *Stagecoach* the summit of the form, an example of "classic maturity," before going on to see in Anthony Mann's early small Westerns the path of further progress. Although there is a certain logic in searching for films at the center of the spectrum, I suspect it is a false one and can see little value in it. Wherever definitions of *the* genre movie have been advanced they have become the weapons of generalization. Insisting on the purity of his classical elements, Bazin dismisses "super-westerns" (*Shane*, *High Noon*, *Duel in the Sun*) because of their introduction of interests "not endemic." Warshow's position is similar, although his conception of the form is narrower, a particular kind of moral and physical texture embodied in his famous but inadequate view of the hero as "the last gentleman." Elsewhere Mann's films have been faulted for their neurotic qualities, strange and powerful works such as *Rancho Notorious* have been refused entry because they are somehow "not westerns." This impulse may well be informed by a fear that unless the form is defined precisely (which inevitably excludes) it will disappear, wraithlike, from under our eyes. The call has echoed out over the lonely landscape of critical endeavor: what *is* the Western?

The model we must hold before us is of a varied and flexible structure, a thematically fertile and ambiguous world of historical material shot through with archetypal elements which are themselves ever in flux. In defining the five basic modes of literary fiction Northrop Frye has described myth as stories about gods; romance as a world in which men are superior both to other men and to their environment; high mimetic where the hero is a leader but subject to social criticism and natural law; low mimetic where the hero is one of us; and ironic where the hero is inferior to ourselves and we look down on the absurdity of his plight. If we borrow this scale, it quickly becomes apparent that if the Western was originally rooted between romance and high mimetic (characteristic forms of which are epic and tragedy), it rapidly became open to inflection in any direction. Surely the only definition we can advance of the Western hero, for example, is that he is both complete and incomplete, serene and growing, vulnerable and invulnerable, a man and a god. If at juvenile levels the action approaches the near-divine, for serious artists who understand the tensions within the genre the focus

can be anywhere along the scale. The directors I examine in detail later are good examples: in Anthony Mann there is a constant drive toward mythic quality in the hero; in Sam Peckinpah there is a rich creative play with the romantic potential; with Budd Boetticher it is the ironic mode that dominates.

The romantic mainstream that the Western took on from pulp literature provided it with the stately ritual of displaced myth, the movement of a godlike figure into the demonic wasteland, the death and resurrection, the return to a paradisal garden. Within the form were to be found seminal archetypes common to all myth, the journey and the quest, the ceremonies of love and marriage, food and drink, the rhythms of waking and sleeping, life and death. But the incursions of melodrama and revenge had turned the form on its axis, the structure torn in the directions of both morality play and tragedy. Overlaying and interpenetrating the historical thematic was an archetypal and metaphysical ideology as well. Manifest destiny was answered by divine providence, a classical conception of fate brooding over the sins of man. Where history was localizing and authenticating archetype, archetype was stiffening and universalizing history.

The Western thus was—and is—a

complex variable, its peculiar alchemy allowing a wide range of intervention, choice and experiment by script-writer and director. History provides a source of epics, spectacle and action films, pictures sympathetic to the Indian, "realistic" films, even anti-Westerns (Delmer Daves's *Cowboy*). From the archetypal base flow revenge films, fables, tragedies, pastorals, and a juvenile stream of product. But of course the dialectic is always at work and the elements are never pure. Much that is produced, the great bulk of it inevitably undistinguished, occupies a blurred middle ground. But for the artist of vision in *rapport* with the genre, it offers a great freedom for local concentration and imaginative play.

"My name is John Ford. I make Westerns." Few film-makers can have been so serene about accepting such a label. After all, the industry must have ambivalent attitudes about the "horse-opera" which has been their bread and butter for so long. And of course the Western has been at the heart of mass culture, the staple of television, its motifs decorating advertisements and politicians, the pulp fiction and comic books flowing endlessly as do the films themselves. But in fact its greatest strength has been this very pervasiveness and repetition. In this context, the Western appears a

huge iceberg: the small tip of which has been the province of criticism, the great undifferentiated and submerged body below principally agitating the social critic, the student of mass media, the educationalist. This sharp division has been unfortunate: sociology and education have often taken up crude positions in their obliviousness to the highest achievements; criticism has failed to explore the dialectic that keeps the form vigorous. For if mass production at the base exploits the peak, the existence of that base allows refinement and reinvigoration. It is only because the Western has been everywhere before us for so long that it "works." For over the years a highly sophisticated sublanguage of the cinema has been created that is intuitively understood by the audience, a firm basis for art.

It is not just that in approaching the Western a director has a structure that is saturated with conceptual significance: the core of meanings is in the imagery itself. Through usage and time, recurring elements anchored in the admixture of history and archetype and so central as to be termed *structural*—the hero, the antagonist, the community, landscape—have taken on an everpresent cluster of possible significances. To see a church in a movie—any film but a Western—is to see a church; the camera records. By working carefully for it a film-maker can give that church meaning, through visual emphasis, context, repetitions, dialogue. But a church in a Western has *a priori* a potential expressiveness rooted in the accretions of the past. In Ford's *My Darling Clementine* a half-built church appears in one brief scene: yet it embodies the spirit of pioneer America. Settlers dance vigorously on the rough planks in the open air, the flag fluttering above the frame of the church perched precariously on the edge of the desert. Marching ceremoniously up the incline toward them, the camera receding with an audacious stateliness, come Tombstone's knight and his "lady fair," Wyatt Earp and Clementine. The community members are ordered aside by the elder as the couple move on to the floor, their robust dance marking the marriage ceremony that unites the best qualities of East and West. It is one of Ford's great moments.

However, the scene is not magic, but flows from an exact understanding (or intuition) of how time-honored elements can have the resonance of an *icon*. This term, which I borrow from art history, should connote an image that both records and carries a conceptual and emotional weight drawn from a *defined* symbolic field, a tradition. Like Scripture, the Western offers a world of metaphor, a range of

latent content that can be made manifest depending on the film-maker's awareness and preoccupations. Thus in Boetticher's *Decision at Sundown* a marriage ceremony is completely violated by the hero who promises to kill the bridegroom by nightfall. Here the meaning flows completely from the players, in particular Randolph Scott's irrational behavior; the church itself is devoid of meaning. In Anthony Mann churches rarely appear. In Peckinpah churches have been a saloon and a brothel, and religion in characters has masked a damaging repressiveness. If we turn to the Indian we find that, apart from the early *Seminole*, he functions in Boetticher as part of a hostile universe, no more and no less. In Mann, however, the Indian is part of the natural order and as such his slaughter stains the landscape; it is not surprising that at times he comes, like an avenging spirit, to redress the balance. In Peckinpah the Indian, ushering in the theme of savagery, brings us to the very center of the director's world.

Central to much that I have been saying is the principle of convention. I have refrained from using the term only because it is often loosely used and might have confused the issues. At times the term is used pejoratively, implying cliché; at others it is employed to invoke a set of mystical rules that the master of the form can juggle. In this light, a Western is a Western is a Western. If we see the term more neutrally, as an area of agreement between audience and artist with reference to the form which his art will take, it might prove useful at this stage to recapitulate the argument by summarizing the interrelated aspects of the genre that I have tried to isolate, all of which are in some measure conventional.

(a) History: The basic convention of the genre is that films in Western guise are about America's past. This constant tension with history and the freedom it extends to script-writer and film-maker to choose their distance is a great strength.

(b) Themes: The precise chronology of the genre and its inheritance of contradictions fundamental to the American mind dictate a rich range of themes expressed through a series of familiar character types and conflicts (e.g. law versus the gun, sheep versus cattle). These motifs, situations and characters can be the focus for a director's interests or can supply the ground from which he will quarry what concerns him.

(c) Archetype: The inherent complexity and structural confusion (or the *decadence*) of the pulp literature tradition that the Western drew on from the beginning meant that Westerns could incorporate elements of ro-

mance, tragedy, comedy, morality play. By a process of natural commercial selection cycles emerged and began to establish a range of forms.

(d) Icons: As a result of mass production, the accretions of time, and the dialectic of history and archetype, characters, situations and actions can have an emblematic power. Movement on the horizon, the erection of a community, the pursuit of Indians, these have a range of possible associations. Scenes such as passing on gun-lore, bathing or being barbered, playing poker, have a latent ritualistic meaning which can be brought to the surface and inflected. The quest, the journey, the confrontation, these can take on moral or allegorical overtones.

What holds all of these elements together (and in that sense provides the basic convention) is narrative and dramatic structure. It is only through mastery of these that a film-maker can both engage his audience and order the form in a personally meaningful way. At a general level this means the understanding and control necessary for any expression of emotion in terms of film—the creating of fear, suspense, amusement, awe. However, with an art as popular as the Western this must also mean a precise awareness of audience expectation with reference to a range of characters—

preeminently hero and antagonist—
and testing situations, conflicts, spectacle, landscape, physical action and
violence. Fundamental to success
would seem to be the understanding
that the world created must be essentially fabulous. While treating situations that have their relevance for us,
the form must not impinge too directly on our experience. The world
that the film creates is self-contained
and its own; it comments not on our
life but on the actions and relationships it reveals to us. So long as the
world evoked is *other*, few limitations
exist. A commonplace about the
form, that it is handy for exploring
simple moral issues, does not survive
the experience of attending to any
number of works: the maturity of relationships in Robert Parrish's *Wonderful Country*, the complex moral
and metaphysical rhetoric of *Johnny*
Guitar, the work, certainly, of the
three directors studied in this book,
these could hardly be called simple.
Nor are social and psychological elements impossible so long as they are
held in fruitful tension with the romantic thrust of the genre. *Showdown*
at Boot Hill, where Charles Bronson
has become a bounty hunter because
he feels he is too *short*, is an un-
successful Freudian tale. *The Left-*
handed Gun, where the murder of a
father-figure turns Billy the Kid anti-
social and self-destructive, is a distinguished psychological tragedy. *3.10 to*
Yuma and *Shane*, both maligned because of their success where the genre
proper fails (i.e., with most film journalists), are honorable works. Rather
than dogma, the grounds must be
quality. And the challenge always is
to find the dramatic structure that best
serves both film-maker and audience.

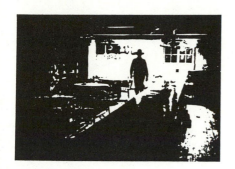

Filmography
Bibliography

Ford Filmography, 1930–1966

The list that follows cites only the script writer and script source for Ford's feature films since 1930 and includes the original American publisher and publication date for each source. A complete filmography of John Ford is available in Peter Bogdanovich's *John Ford* (Berkeley: University of California Press, 1974); another filmography, based on Bogdanovich, appears in Andrew Sinclair's *John Ford* (New York: Dial Press, 1979).

1930 *Men Without Women*
Script: Dudley Nichols. Based on the story "Submarine" by John Ford and James K. McGuiness.

1930 *Born Reckless*
Script: Dudley Nichols. Based on the novel *Louis Beretti* by Donald

Henderson Clarke (New York: The Vanguard Press, 1929).

1930 *Up the River*
Script: Maurine Watkins (and, uncredited, John Ford and William Collier, Sr.). Based on a story by Watkins.

1931 *Seas Beneath*
Script: Dudley Nichols. Based on a story by James Parker, Jr.

1931 *The Brat*
Script: Sonya Levien, S. N. Behrman, and Maude Fulton. Based on the play *The Brat* by Maude Fulton (New York: Longmans Green & Co., 1926).

1931 *Arrowsmith*
Script: Sidney Howard. Based on the novel *Arrowsmith* by Sinclair Lewis (New York: Harcourt, Brace, 1925).

1932 *Air Mail*
Script: Dale Van Every and Frank Wead. Based on a story by Frank Wead.

1932 *Flesh*
Script: Leonard Praskins and Edgar Allen Woolf. Based on a story by Edmund Goulding.

1933 *Pilgrimage*
Script: Philip Klein and Barry Connors. Based on the story "Pilgrimage" by I. A. R. (Ida Alena Ross) Wylie, *American Magazine*, November 1932.

1933 *Dr. Bull*
Script: Paul Green. Based on the novel *The Last Adam* by James Gould Cozzens (New York: Harcourt, Brace, 1933).

1934 *The Lost Patrol*
Script: Dudley Nichols and Garrett Fort. Based on the story "Patrol" by Philip MacDonald, published in *Patrol* (New York: Harper Bros., 1928).

1934 *The World Moves On*
Script: Reginald C. Berkeley.

1934 *Judge Priest*
Script: Dudley Nichols and Lamar Trotti. Based on stories by Irvin S. Cobb.

1935 *The Whole Town's Talking*
Script: Jo Swerling. Based on the novel *Jailbreak* by W. R. Burnett, published in *Colliers*, July & August, 1934.

1935 *The Informer*
Script: Dudley Nichols. Based on the novel *The Informer* by Liam O'Flaherty (New York: Knopf, 1925).

1935 *Steamboat Round the Bend*
Script: Dudley Nichols and Lamar Trotti. Based on the novel *Steamboat Round the Bend* by Ben Lucian Burman (New York: Farrar & Rinehart, 1933).

1936 *The Prisoner of Shark Island*
Script: Nunnally Johnson. Based on the life of Dr. Samuel A. Mudd.

1936 *Mary of Scotland*
Script: Dudley Nichols. Based on the play *Mary of Scotland* by Maxwell Anderson (Garden City, N.Y.: Doubleday, Doran & Co., 1934).

1936 *The Plough and the Stars*
Script: Dudley Nichols. Based on the play *The Plough and the Stars* by Sean O'Casey (New York: Macmillan Co., 1926).

1937 *Wee Willie Winkie*
Script: Ernest Pascal and Julian Josephson. Based on the story "Wee

Willie Winkie" by Rudyard Kipling
(New York: G. Monro's Sons, 1888).

1937 *The Hurricane*
Script: Dudley Nichols. Based on the
novel *The Hurricane* by Charles
Nordhoff (Boston: Little, Brown,
1936).

1938 *Four Men and a Prayer*
Script: Richard Sherman, Sonya
Levien, and Walter Ferris. Based on
the novel *Four Men and a Prayer* by
David Garth (New York: H. C. Kinsey
& Co., 1937).

1938 *Submarine Patrol*
Script: Rian James, Darrell Ware, and
Jack Yellen. Based on the novel
Splinter Fleet by Ray Milholland
(Indianapolis: Bobbs Merrill, 1936).

1939 *Stagecoach*
Script: Dudley Nichols. Based on the
story "Stage to Lordsburg" by Ernest
Haycox, published in *Collier's*, April
10, 1937.

1939 *Young Mr. Lincoln*
Script: Lamar Trotti. Based on the life
of Abraham Lincoln.

1939 *Drums Along the Mohawk*
Script: Lamar Trotti and Sonya
Levien. Based on the novel *Drums
Along the Mohawk* by Walter D.
Edmonds (Boston: Little, Brown,
1936).

1940 *The Grapes of Wrath*
Script: Nunnally Johnson. Based on
the novel *The Grapes of Wrath* by
John Steinbeck (New York: Viking
Press, 1939).

1940 *The Long Voyage Home*
Script: Dudley Nichols. Based on four
one-act plays (*The Moon of the
Caribbees*, *In The Zone*, *Bound East
for Cardiff*, *The Long Voyage Home*)
by Eugene O'Neill, published in *The
Moon of the Caribbees and Six Other
Plays of the Sea* (New York: Boni &
Liveright, Inc. 1923).

1941 *Tobacco Road*
Script: Nunnally Johnson. Based on
the play *Tobacco Road* by Jack
Kirkland (New York: Viking Press,
1934) and on the novel of the same
name by Erskine Caldwell (New
York: Charles Scribner's Sons, 1932).

1941 *How Green Was My Valley*
Script: Philip Dunne. Based on the
novel *How Green Was My Valley* by
Richard Llewellyn (New York:
Macmillan Co., 1940).

1945 *They Were Expendable*
Script: Frank W. Wead. Based on the
book *They Were Expendable* by
William L. White (Cleveland: World
Publishing Co., 1942).

1946 *My Darling Clementine*
Script: Samuel G. Engel and Winston

Miller. Based on the book *Wyatt Earp, Frontier Marshal* by Stuart N. Lake (Boston: Houghton Mifflin Co., 1931).

1947 *The Fugitive*
Script: Dudley Nichols. Based on the novel *The Power and the Glory* by Graham Greene (London: W. Heinemann Ltd., 1940; American edition *The Labyrinthine Ways*, New York: Viking Press, 1940).

1948 *Fort Apache*
Script: Frank Nugent. Based on the story "Massacre" by James Warner Bellah, published in *The Saturday Evening Post*, February 22, 1947.

1948 *Three Godfathers*
Script: Laurence Stallings and Frank Nugent. Based on the story *Three Godfathers* by Peter B. Kyne (New York: George B. Doran Co., 1913).

1949 *She Wore a Yellow Ribbon*
Script: Laurence Stallings and Frank Nugent. Based on the story "War Party" by James Warner Bellah, published in *The Saturday Evening Post*, June 19, 1948.

1950 *When Willie Comes Marching Home*
Script: Mary Loos and Richard Sale. Based on the story "When Leo Comes Marching Home" by Sy Gomberg, published in *Collier's*, May 12, 1945.

1950 *Wagon Master*
Script: Frank Nugent and Patrick Ford.

1950 *Rio Grande*
Script: James K. McGuinness. Based on the story "Mission with No Record" by James Warner Bellah, published in *The Saturday Evening Post*, September 17, 1947.

1952 *What Price Glory*
Script: Phoebe and Henry Ephron. Based on the play *What Price Glory* by Maxwell Anderson and Laurence Stallings, published in *Three American Plays* by Anderson and Stallings (New York: Harcourt, Brace, 1927).

1952 *The Quiet Man*
Script: Frank Nugent. Based on the story "The Quiet Man" by Maurice Walsh, published in *Take Your Choice* (Philadelphia: J. P. Lippincott, 1954).

1953 *The Sun Shines Bright*
Script: Laurence Stallings. Based on three stories by Irvin S. Cobb: "The Sun Shines Bright," published in *Down Yonder with Judge Priest and Irvin S. Cobb* (New York: Long & Smith, Inc., 1932); "The Mob From Massac," published in *Back Home* (New York: George H. Doran Co., 1912); "The Lord Provides," published in *Old Judge Priest* (Garden City, N.Y.: Doubleday, Doran & Co., 1932).

1953 *Mogambo*
Script: John Lee Mahin. Based on the play *Red Dust* by Wilson Collison. Unpublished; produced on Broadway, January 2, 1928; filmed as *Red Dust* (1932).

1955 *The Long Gray Line*
Script: Edward Hope. Based on the autobiography of Marty Maher, *Bringing Up the Brass*, by Marty Maher and Nardi Reeder Campion (New York: McKay, 1951).

1955 *Mister Roberts*
Script: Frank Nugent and Joshua Logan. Based on the play *Mister Roberts* by Joshua Logan and Thomas Heggen (New York: Random House, 1948) and on the novel of the same name by Heggen (Boston: Houghton Mifflin, 1946).

1956 *The Searchers*
Script: Frank Nugent. Based on the novel *The Searchers* by Alan LeMay (New York: Harper & Row, 1954).

1957 *The Wings of Eagles*
Script: Frank Fenton and William Wister Haines. Based on the life and writings of Commander Frank W. Wead, USN.

1957 *The Rising of the Moon*
Script: Frank Nugent. Based on the story "The Majesty of the Law" by Frank O'Connor, published in *Bones of Contention* (New York: Macmillan Co., 1936); the play *A Minute's Wait* by Michael J. McHugh (Dublin: Duffy, 1922); the play *The Rising of the Moon* by Lady Gregory (Dublin: Mainsel, 1909).

1958 *The Last Hurrah*
Script: Frank Nugent. Based on the novel *The Last Hurrah* by Edwin O'Connor (Boston: Little, Brown, 1956).

1959 *Gideon of Scotland Yard*
Script: T. E. B. Clarke. Based on the novel *Gideon's Day* by J. J. Marric (pseudonym for John Creasey) (New York: Harper & Row, 1955).

1959 *The Horse Soldiers*
Script: John Lee Mahin and Martin Rackin. Based on the novel *The Horse Soldiers* by Harold Sinclair (New York: Harper & Row, 1956).

1960 *Sergeant Rutledge*
Script: Willis Goldbeck and James Warner Bellah.

1961 *Two Rode Together*
Script: Frank Nugent. Based on the novel *Comanche Captives* by Will Cook (New York: Bantam, 1960).

1962 *The Man Who Shot Liberty Valance*
Script: Willis Goldbeck and James Warner Bellah. Based on the story "The Man Who Shot Liberty Valance"

by Dorothy M. Johnson, published in *Indian Country* (New York: Ballantine Books, 1953).

1963 *Donovan's Reef*
Script: Frank Nugent and James E. Grant. Based on a story by Edmund Belion, adapted by James Michener.

1964 *Cheyenne Autumn*
Script: James R. Webb. Based on the book *Cheyenne Autumn* by Mari Sandoz (New York: McGraw-Hill, 1953).

1966 *Seven Women*
Script: Janet Green and John McCormick. Based on the story "Chinese Finale" by Norah Lofts, published in *I Met A Gypsy* (New York: Knopf, 1935).

Selected Bibliography

Anderson, Lindsay. "John Ford." *Cinema (Beverly Hills)* 6 (1971): 21–36.

Baxter, John. *The Cinema of John Ford*. The International Film Guide Series. New York: A. S. Barnes & Co., 1971.

Bazin, Andre. "The Western: Or the American Film Par Excellence." Trans. Hugh Gray. In *What Is Cinema?* vol. 2 , pp. 140–48. Berkeley: University of California Press, 1971.

Bogdanovich, Peter. *John Ford*. Rev. ed. Berkeley: University of California Press, 1978.

Budd, Michael. "A Home in the Wilderness: Visual Imagery in John Ford's Westerns." *Cinema Journal* 16 (1976):62–75.

Cawelti, John G. *The Six-Gun Mystique*. Bowling Green, Ohio: Bowling Green University Popular Press, 1971.

Fenin, George N., and William K. Everson. *The Western: From Silents to the Seventies*. New York: Grossman Publishers, 1973.

Fleischer, Stefan. "A Study through Stills of *My Darling Clementine*." *Journal of Modern Literature* 3 (1973):246–52.

French, Phillip. *Westerns: Aspects of a Movie Genre*. Rev. ed. New York: Oxford University Press, 1977.

Kennedy, Burt. "A Talk with John Ford." *Action* 3 (Sept.–Oct., 1968):6–8.

Kitses, Jim. *Horizons West*. Cinema One Series, 12. Bloomington: Indiana University Press, 1970.

Lake, Stuart N. *Wyatt Earp, Frontier Marshal*. Boston: Houghton Mifflin Co., 1931.

Libby, Bill. "The Old Wrangler Rides Again." *Cosmopolitan* (March 1964), pp. 13–21.

McBride, Joseph, and Michael Wilmington. *John Ford*. New York: Da Capo Press, 1975.

Mitry, Jean. "Rencontre avec John Ford." *Cahiers du Cinéma* (March 1955); reprinted in *Interviews with Film Directors*, ed. Andrew Sarris. New York: Bobbs Merrill, 1966.

Nachbar, Jack, ed. *Focus on the Western*. Englewood Cliffs, N.J.: Prentice-Hall, 1974.

Place, J. A. *The Western Films of John Ford*. Secaucus, N.J.: Citadel Press, 1974.

Sarris, Andrew. *The John Ford Movie Mystery*. Cinema One Series, 27. Bloomington: Indiana University Press, 1975.

Sinclair, Andrew. *John Ford*. New York: Dial Press, 1979.

Stowell, H. Peter. "John Ford's Literary Sources: From Realism to Romance." *Literature/Film Quarterly* 5 (1977):164–73.

Tavernier, Bertrand. "John Ford à Paris." *Positif* 82 (March 1967): 7–21.

Tavernier, Claudine. "La Quatrième Dimension de la Vieillesse." *Cinéma 69* 137 (1969):32–49.

Wollen, Peter. "The Auteur Theory." In *Signs and Meanings in the Cinema*. Cinema One Series, 9. Bloomington: Indiana University Press, 1972.